Banish Clutter Forever

How The Toothbrush Principle Will Change Your Life

SHEILA CHANDRA

Vermilion

LONDON

9 10 8

Published in 2010 by Vermilion, an imprint of Ebury Publishing
A Random House Group Company

Copyright © Sheila Chandra 2010

Sheila Chandra has asserted her right to be identified
as the author of this Work in accordance with the
Copyright, Designs and Patents Act 1988

All rights reserved. No part of this publication may be
reproduced, stored in a retrieval system, or transmitted in any
form or by any means, electronic, mechanical, photocopying,
recording or otherwise, without the prior permission
of the copyright owner

The Random House Group Limited Reg. No. 954009

Addresses for companies within the Random House Group can be
found at www.randomhouse.co.uk

A CIP catalogue record for this book
is available from the British Library

ISBN 9780091935023

To buy books by your favourite authors and register for offers
visit www.randomhouse.co.uk

The Random House Group Limited supports The Forest Stewardship
Council® (FSC®), the leading international forest-certification organisation.
Our books carrying the FSC label are printed on FSC®-certified paper.
FSC is the only forest-certification scheme supported by the leading
environmental organisations, including Greenpeace. Our
paper procurement policy can be found at
www.randomhouse.co.uk/environment

MIX
Paper from
responsible sources
FSC
www.fsc.org   FSC® C016897

Printed and bound in Great Britain by Clays Ltd, St Ives plc

For Sue Roberts,
without whom I'd never have thought
to become an author

About the author

Sheila Chandra is a new author but has been a successful singer and songwriter for 28 years with 10 albums to her credit. Her first single was in the Top Ten in various countries around the world. Since then she has become well known as a pioneer in the World Music genre. She manages herself, runs her own music publishing and production companies, and oversees all aspects of her career: consequently she fully understands the challenges of remaining organised and disciplined whilst working from home, and benefits enormously from living and working in a harmonious environment.

Contents

Introduction   xi

1. What is the toothbrush principle?   1
2. Bathrooms   15
3. Your vision   25
4. So what's stopping you?   39
5. Myths and bad habits   61
6. Getting started with good habits   81
7. Storage spaces   95
8. Bedrooms   105
9. Kitchens   125
10. Living spaces   137
11. The home office part 1   151
12. The home office part 2   193
13. Maintenance and troubleshooting   213
14. A final word   229

Appendix I: Five ways to build a new mindset   231
Appendix II: The 5 principles to apply to clearing   233
Acknowledgements   237

Introduction

Have you always wanted to be one of the glamorous people in those 'lifestyle' ads? The ones who look flawless and exist in a perfect, comfortable and luxurious environment? They always seem to be relaxing, don't they? Or perhaps your dreams are more modest? Do you just wish that the physical chaos in your house wasn't making it so hard for you to get the simplest thing done? Do both of these visions of your possible future seem impossible to reach?

Living in a well-organised and even very tidy space, all the time, without spending huge amounts of time maintaining it, is not just possible, but is actually easier and less stressful than living in chaos. Yes, read that sentence again. Not just possible, but once you have the principles in place, it is *EASIER*. I know, because I have lived that way for many years and helped many of my friends to do so too. I wasn't born knowing how to do that, either. There is no such thing as having a 'tidy gene'. Tidiness (or the ability to be well organised - things don't have to look tidy if you don't want them to) is a skill that is usually unconsciously learned but it can also be consciously acquired whatever age you are. I discovered how to do that and I've set out all the principles I discovered here for you, in the easiest system possible. Perhaps you don't believe that I was ever messy. Or perhaps you think your mess is just far worse than I can imagine. Not so. Here is a little of my story.

I grew up in an incredibly untidy and inefficient household. Both the systems for organising time and for organising things were very chaotic. As a child, I wondered how other people managed to live differently.

I lived with my extended family in an old and crumbling Victorian house. We had originally rented one floor and gradually taken over another. One whole room on that top floor – one of the biggest, lightest rooms in the house – was filled from floor to ceiling with junk and furniture. As long as I could remember no one had gone into it, although I had peeped into it once. I longed to know what was in there. I imagined, as a seven-year-old, that I would find some treasure that had been overlooked. I wanted to have an adventure in it and I was sure that the tangle of furniture legs would be my Amazonian forest.

Money was very, very tight in my family. We rented that draughty, broken-down and difficult-to-keep-clean house with lead pipes, broken sash windows and peeling paint. As a child I thought that the reason that our household felt so chaotic was the fact that the house was so bad. When the council decided to knock the whole block down and promised to re-house us in a newly refurbished home, I dreamed of having my own room instead of sharing a bed in a sort of bed/sitting room with my mother and my younger sister. I dreamed of privacy, and most of all, I dreamed of living in a beautiful and tidy space.

My mother had stored away umpteen things that were 'too good to use now' with the promise that we would use them in the new house. I hated the chaos. I hated the way I could never find anything. I hated the way it wasn't safe to put something down because someone would move it and you'd have to spend hours looking for it. I hated the way we put things by and never enjoyed the good things we had. I was sure this wouldn't happen in the new house – the new house was to be the promised land.

When I was 12, the council finally fulfilled their promise, and a couple of very surprising things happened. First of all, the day I had waited for, when I could explore the junk room, never came. My mother never even unlocked it. Who knows what was in there? She just couldn't face sorting it out and left everything to be destroyed and taken away with the rubble. She had told me it was full of antiques, and as the room had got filled up in the 1960s, when many people sold their old-fashioned furniture for peanuts, it quite possibly was. We were never given the chance to benefit from their use or from their sale because she was overwhelmed with our other, very tatty possessions.

The other interesting thing that happened was that when we finally got to our new home, there was a room for everyone. However, my mother filled her room with spare furniture and other items and moved into my room. So my room was never beautiful or tidy or coordinated. I was very disappointed. I noticed that other family members also compulsively filled their bedrooms with junk that they never used ... to the point where there was hardly any floor space. The cellar was packed; the attics were packed; the cupboards were bursting. It was as chaotic as ever, even though we had had a fresh start, within three months of moving in.

This was my first lesson about clutter, although I didn't know it at the time. Clutter isn't caused by lack of time or space, but by indecision and the lack of a good system. It builds itself to match the exact blueprint inside the head of the person whose home it is, in the same way as a builder will lay one brick on top of another according to the architect's plans. In my mother's case, she also had a layer of myths and resistances (part of her emotional clutter) that stopped her ever changing her mindset and finding better ways to organise things. One of the purposes of this book is to build new and efficient blueprints for you so that your well-organised space stays that way easily.

Despite the fact that this chaotic household is the one I grew up in, today I'm self-employed, work from home, travel a lot for business purposes, and I've learned step-by-step how to organise my house, my business and my time properly in order to survive. I want you to know that I've seen clutter (and the dirt it can collect) far worse than yours and lived in it, and I've learned very consciously how to stop creating it. You can learn to do that too, whatever your inherited patterns are.

I rarely lose anything, forget appointments, or miss deadlines. My house is very tidy most of the time. And I hardly ever spend more than 10 minutes a day tidying up. Most days, I don't tidy up at all. Okay, I live alone, but it wasn't that different when I was married. If you are a Mum, or self-employed, I would guess you already manage a minor miracle in scheduling. Being tidy as well probably seems like one step too far. But think of the long-term benefits if you took it on. Wouldn't your life run more smoothly, your house be easier to clean, and far nicer to invite friends to and relax in when your children are in bed, or your work is done at the end of the day? Wouldn't there be less stress and less expense if things were where you expected to find them and not broken, dirty or lost? Wouldn't you have more time to do what you love, or to focus on the really important things in your life, if you weren't holding the mess back all the time? But I'm guessing that you don't have a way to create this at the moment, do you? Well, I'd like to help.

I think I have the answers you need. I have developed a really simple system here that I have been sharing with my friends for years. It is one that will help you to solve your own individual recurring clutter jams, whether they're on the scale of a nudge in a car park or a four-lane pile-up.

How to use this book

I recommend that you read the first two chapters of this book to get a feel for the method, and try out the bathroom exercise in Chapter 2 before you go any further. That will be the quickest way for you to see how effectively this approach can work for you. Reading the next four chapters and the maintenance and troubleshooting chapter will help you to banish any inherited tendencies you have to create clutter. Once you understand the basic principles, however, this book is designed to be held in your hand, if necessary, and to 'talk' you through the process in each specific room as you start clearing out. It is not obligatory that you clear rooms in the order that the chapters are arranged in but it is recommended, especially if you are new to being organised, have trouble letting things go, or if you have the whole house to sort out.

This isn't a book of hints and tips on how to get organised, and it won't work if you try the method out in a piecemeal fashion in any particular area you've decided to clear. It isn't a quick fix and if you want to keep your home clutter-free, you will need patience while you give yourself time to absorb the new ways of thinking you will have to adopt. On the other hand, once you've mastered the method, you won't find yourself having to have huge 'crash-diet' type clear-outs, which only last for a short time, any more. And you won't need to spend lots of time every day tidying up. This simple system will enable you to live clutter-free, forever.

Chapter one
What is the toothbrush principle?

Something I noticed that was common to most people who live in utter chaos with all their junk was this: they wanted to be different, they were ashamed of their mess, but they didn't know how to change. When the mess got too much, they tidied up, and for a day or so that was the way it stayed. Then one of two things would happen: either they would need something that was right at the back of the cupboard and have to pull everything out to get it and be so fed up or in a hurry that they didn't put it back or, you've guessed it, they wouldn't be able to remember where it was. In 24 hours the mess would be back and they'd have given up in disgust. Tidying up without a larger system in mind is much like crash dieting – it looks very good in the short-term, but it doesn't solve the problem in the long-term.

Something else I noticed though was this. I'd never come across one of them who ever lost their toothbrush. Or had to 'tidy it away'! Their instinct to create a system that was efficient and easy to maintain around something really essential and basic like brushing their teeth was already automatic for them. Similarly, with their tea mugs, kettle, milk and sugar. I have hardly ever been to a house, however chaotic and messy, where the person inviting me has not been able to find the ingredients to make me a cup of tea in five minutes! Why? Because these systems are essential, and because they are pretty standard from house to house, therefore our clutterholics had learned them. But these systems also contain every principle you'll ever need to make your house well organised *and to keep it well organised,* effortlessly. That is the crucial piece of information that you may have been missing. What I am trying to say is, *you already know how to do this!*

'Well organised' versus 'tidy'

I use the words 'well organised' advisedly. I didn't say tidy. You can use this system to be tidy if you wish. It will work in the most modern and minimalist of homes, but the point is that you may not wish to. If you like having 'knick-knacks' and lots of visual clutter around the place and it makes you feel good, fair enough, why not? Human beings seem to fall into two categories in this regard. Those who like visual 'quietness' in order to think well, and those who function better with a bit of visual stimulus. Neither one of these preferences is superior to the other. They are simply a reflection of your temperament. The people who like visual quietness experience clutter as a competing 'noise' and it is as unpleasant to them as having a siren going off whilst they are trying to talk to you. Others can feel miserable without a bit of 'cosy' stimulation via their visual sense.

I am not suggesting that you become tidy if you don't want to, or that you sort out any room that (however junk filled) you are happy to live in, as it is. This book has solutions that are designed to make your house serve you better. Serve *you*. This is the point which most clutterholics forget. The reason to sort your possessions out is so that your house enables you to get on with doing what you love to do. Wouldn't that feel great?

You bought your home (or rented it). You work to pay the mortgage (or rent). You clean it and maintain it. Shouldn't it work just as hard to make you feel good? It can do so much more than merely shelter you. It can also be an inspiring space that nurtures you and provides a good backdrop for you to enjoy yourself. At the very least it should be organised in a way that allows you to do your daily and weekly tasks quickly and easily. Sounds a bit one-way otherwise, doesn't it?

So what is the principle?

Think about what you do when you move house. I should imagine that one of the first things you unpack is your toothbrush. It's the same when you check into a hotel. You put your toilette or wash bag by the sink. You set this system up in some form immediately even if, in the rest of the hotel room, it looks like a hurricane has hit your luggage. When you moved into your current house, on day one, you unpacked your tooth mug and put your toothbrush and toothpaste in it right by the sink in your bathroom. And there it has stayed ever since. How were you able to set up such an effective system so quickly? I know it sounds daft and incredibly simple but I want you to look at how that simple system works.

Why did you put the tooth mug, toothbrush and tooth-paste by the sink? Because you have a task to do every day that requires those three items, and only those. You put them by the sink so that everything you needed for the task would be within arm's reach of where the task has to be performed. And the crucial factor here is that because every-thing you needed was within arm's length of where you do the task, it was easy to replace them there without thinking.

Think about that for a minute. You are never tempted to put your toothbrush down somewhere else, are you? You never throw it in the bath for now and put the tooth-paste on the toilet cistern and vow to tidy them up later, and then lose one or other of them in the meantime. You never forget where your toothbrush belongs and put it down somewhere random because you don't have time to, or can't find, a space for it now. But there are many other items that you regularly put down in random places, and lose, and make the tasks you need to accomplish with them hard to complete. You aren't making it easy for yourself to be as tidy with them as you are with your toothbrush, and this is where the problem with your current system lies.

But let's go back to your incredible success. You have maintained, here, one tiny but perfectly organised and efficient system, all your life, with virtually no thought whatsoever. You learned it as a child, and you maintained it because as an adult when you left home you made the pragmatic decision that other people would only want to know you if your teeth were clean and consequently your breath was fresh. Even the most diehard clutter collectors learn this system and use it. But the trouble is, they never look at how it evolved, or why it works. They never look at it as a principle, just as a 'thing you do'. And so they miss the way in which it could apply to every other thing in their house and help them to stay well organised, just as effortlessly.

So how and why does it work?

What you automatically do with your toothbrush actually involves two concepts: 'Zoning' and 'Completion'. They are interlinked and it is hard to get tidy and stay tidy without *both* of them in place together. This is why that 'blitz' tidying you do before your friends come round doesn't last. Let's look at these two ideas more closely.

■ Zoning

This concept involves placing things needed for a particular task where they will be used. Ideally as close to that place as possible. This means that you are more likely to replace them correctly without thinking after you have finished with them, since you are already there, and, of course, you find them easily next time you need to do that particular task. Notice I didn't say place 'like with like'. That can look logical but actually trip you up. I don't put all my beauty products together in the bathroom. I put each one exactly where I use it – that's tidier than it sounds.

Human beings are lazy creatures. By that I mean that we all instinctively hate to do things that seem inconveniently laborious to us. In the short term we may avoid the problem but in the long term, our discontent will make us come up with a solution. This is because there is always something far more worthwhile that we would rather be doing. It's a great instinct. The ability to stay in touch with what is important to us, and to minimise the effort we put into the mundane tasks we need to do, is one of the things that makes us so creative, and makes us support each other in our inventiveness.

Think about the washing machine, for example. A machine that, in 40 minutes, can do what it took our great-grandmothers a whole day plus a huge fire, a copper and a mangle to accomplish. 'Wash Day' used to be a major event in every household for centuries, but it was laborious and boring, so eventually we invented an amazingly convenient solution which we can no longer imagine living without.

You are probably far too polite to have imagined this, but I am really lazy. If I didn't put the things I need close to the task at hand, I'd feel as though getting the task done was a struggle. And I'd leave them in random places afterwards because I'd be feeling resentful or even exhausted when I'd finished. Does living in your house feel like a struggle? Is it hard to get started on tasks you need to do? This may be the reason why.

Tidying up isn't going to work unless it is done in line with this principle. Putting something in a cupboard, however neatly, isn't going to work if that item is stored across the room from where it will be used. Or if it is stored in another room altogether... In fact, if that is the way items are arranged in your space it can make your house seem unwelcoming on a gut level. This is the polar opposite of that lovely 'cared for' feeling you get when you walk into a luxury hotel suite and find fresh flowers, fruit, fluffy towels and robes left out for you and the bed turned down. Allowing your home to be arranged in a way that makes it feel like a hostile environment is not good for your self-esteem either. You are giving yourself subliminal messages 20 times a day that your comfort, and therefore you, don't really matter.

When you are finding a good place to store things, apart from proximity to the task, you also have to consider how often you use that particular item. In my kitchen, all those obscure flan cases and cake tins and that specialist wire rack for roasting geese, which I only use once a year or so, are stored in the cupboards that are furthest away from the cooker and main work surfaces or on harder to reach shelves. The more frequently used items, like my omelette pan (I love omelettes!), are stored in front of them where they are more to hand. That is because I am going to reach for my omelette pan three times a month and I will lay my hand on it immediately. I will reach for my cake tins twice a year. If I baked a lot but hated omelettes, this order would have to be reversed.

Imagine what it would be like if, given my liking for omelettes, I reversed the layout and put my omelette pan behind my cake tins. Can you see how many times I would spend five minutes pulling my cake tins out to get the pan, and to put it back when it was washed, and then replace the cake tins? (If I bothered at all to replace them at that point!) That's 15 minutes a month or *three hours* a year! Multiply that number by 10, for just 10 things that are not in their most efficient places and that figure starts to look frightening.

That is why, when the space isn't organised well, most people don't bother to put things back and the clutter starts to take over. This goes for your kids too. They don't have the time. But it also stops them getting organised, because they imagine that tidy people do spend that kind of time being tidy. They don't. They are just as lazy (or rather 'creative', 'inventive' or 'efficient'– whichever word you like to use) as I am. They just knew how to find a good place for the item in the first place, based on an acknowledgement of the fact that they are lazy. This brings me to the second concept which is...

■ Completion
Having the correct materials or equipment to hand doesn't just make it easier to start the task, but also to put things

back just where they will be needed, immediately afterwards. This form of completion needs to become a habit. In fact, ideally, completion should become an addiction that drives you towards replacing things correctly first time, and we will look at ways in which we can help this process along in successive chapters. But it cannot work if the way in which things are arranged in the physical space doesn't help it along. You always knew space and time were linked! (Okay, physics is not my thing...)

So how do I know where to put things, then?

How did the tidy but lazy people know where to put things so that they would be tidy automatically in the first place? The unconscious and 'naturally orderly' blueprint for storing things, which they inherited, told them that the things in a room should be organised, not according to efficient use of space, or by categorising like with like, but by *function*.

Function

You already do this, but you just don't realise it, and you don't apply the principle consistently. The place where you do it automatically is with your furniture. This is because you are compelled to place your furniture according to function and not by the other less useful principles by which I am guessing you store your smaller things.

What would happen if you didn't do this? Well, if you simply wanted to use all the available space efficiently, you would pile your sideboard on top of your sofa, and your TV on top of that. It would take up far less space. But that doesn't serve those items' functions, does it? It makes them impossible to use. And if you used the principle of 'like with like' on your furniture then you would place all the beds together in the largest room in the house. I don't think you'd be very popular if you did that! Especially if your granny was staying…

You'd never do this with your furniture but using these principles with smaller everyday items can hamper you just as much, because they also need to be placed so that they can be used easily. The idea of using space 'efficiently' and placing 'like with like' is only an advantage in spaces that are purely for storage, such as an attic. What people commonly call 'storage' in living spaces, such as a bedroom, is actually a working system that is constantly being utilised and accessed. It's not static in the way that true storage is, and assuming that it's static when you organise it causes chaos. You need to arrange even the smallest things in a living space so that you can use them.

So, if you are going to make your house feel easier to use you need to look again at all the tasks you do and where you want to do them. A 'task', in this instance, doesn't just mean work. It means any function that your house has to fulfil. This can mean watching TV, or sleeping well, or throwing a party. (It is much harder to throw a party if you can't 'find' your dining table beneath all the stuff it's buried under...) And everything in your house, from the largest items to the smallest, needs to be arranged in such a way that you can feel supported in doing those tasks.

Who is the best person to do this? You are. You don't need me, or a clutter-clearing expert (although you might need someone to help out with the sheer volume and to keep you at it). Your house won't support you until you work out what the tasks you do in the house are, and arrange your stuff according to these functions in order of priority. And it won't stay tidy (however beautiful your storage boxes) until you make the habit of 'completion' automatic. *Only you* have this information and power, and so the only person who can do these things is you.

Decision debt

Clutter doesn't usually accumulate because you have too much stuff or too little time. It is most often a reflection of the thousands of tiny decisions you have put off making (about where something should live, or whether it should be thrown out or given away) or haven't known how to make, in the first place. Does being overwhelmed by your stuff and being trapped by it feel like being overweight or in debt? That's because in a way it is. Being overweight or in debt is usually caused by the wish to defer the decision and effort it takes to take control of your health or finances. It is the 'Not now, I will be sensible/sort that out later...' philosophy. Harmless enough, you may think. But when you defer a decision like that, you make a series of small, but opposite decisions by default. And they add up. This is what has happened with your clutter. You are looking at your decision debt. The reason that organising your house feels overwhelming is that each of those decisions is a creditor and all of them are presenting their bills to you at once, and each one of them is going to get in your way in your house until you pay what you owe. It doesn't have to be like that.

Moving into your house (properly)

You have created a debt and clearing it is going to take some effort. Do you remember all the things that you imagined you were going to be able to do when you first thought about living in your current house? Have you done them, and as often as you wanted to?

If your clutter has taken over every room, then in a way, I am going to ask you to move house again. Only it won't cost you anything in removal fees or time spent choosing a new place. I am asking you to move into your house, as you first imagined it, again – properly. It will take some effort and you will have to do it alongside all the hundreds of other things you already have to do in a day. But you've already done it once and your rooms are already basically usable, so it's not going to be that painful. What you are attempting to do is to move into a new way of using your space. This is just as big a move and it will be just as beneficial (if not more so) if you can put the effort in and stick with it. Moreover, you will feel the benefits immediately.

Volume of things

There is one more element of the issue to be dealt with here and it is staring you in the face. That is 'volume of things'. It is likely that you have far more possessions than you use or really need. Your brain can only cope with so much information. The toothbrush principle won't work if essential items are crowded out by junk. This extra stuff also constitutes decisions that you have not yet made. Remember, the way your space looks is a very faithful reflection of the blueprint you have around objects and their storage in your head. If one of your problems is letting go, that will be reflected in your home. The tooth-brush principle is only going to work if you take the time to reassess your mental habits, to make it part of your own thinking and apply it to your own circumstances.

A little less conversation, a little more action...

'Okay, enough talking,' I hear you say. 'Is all this new thinking really worth the effort? Does this principle actually work, and will it work for me?' The next chapter is designed to show you that it does. Rebuilding your attitude to your clutter and establishing a new way of thinking is a fairly big task, but if you want to test the system out first, the next chapter will help you do that, without your needing to understand how you are achieving order. If you want to understand how to apply the toothbrush principle properly then chapters 3, 4, 5 and 6 have the answers you need. The chapters after that will walk you through clearing your rooms step by step and help you to work through any teething problems you may have. First, though, we're going to start with a very simple room to clear and one in which you can get plenty of practice at developing and maintaining good habits.

Chapter two
Bathrooms

The bathroom exercise

Since you have been so phenomenally successful with your system for storing and using your toothbrush, we are going to start right there. All we are going to do is to extend the good habits you have with your toothbrush to the rest of the room. Sounds simple? It is. If you have more than one bathroom, start with the one you use the most.

For this exercise you will need:

- Pen and paper.
- Two plastic storage crates.
- Your usual heavy-duty bathroom cleaning materials.
- A bucket of warm water with a bit of washing-up liquid in it and a cloth for wiping items down as you clear.
- Freshly washed hand towels and, if you can manage it, fresh bath towels for everyone who uses the bathroom.
- Some large bin bags.

This exercise is divided into two parts that can be done on consecutive days and the time should be scheduled into your diary, so that you don't forget to complete it. It should take no more than six hours in total. It can be done much faster than that, but this depends on how much is in your bathroom and whether you can keep a smart pace up. Part 1 should be done all in one go and Part 2 the same, so read through the whole exercise first and remember to allow enough time. Keep moving as fast as you can through each part. Clutter makes you lethargic, so don't let it win! Put on some fast music or get a friend to stand over you and keep you moving if necessary.

The exercise

■ Part 1
Go into the bathroom with your pen and paper.

- List all the people that use it (put each of them on a separate page).
- Under each of their names, make two columns by drawing a line down the centre of the page. In the left-hand column list which toiletries/bathroom accessories (e.g. loofah, shower gel, etc.) they regularly and frequently use. This means daily, or weekly. I know you will be wondering about products you occasionally use. I'm going to be strict here and say if you don't use it at least once a month, either now or in a different season (say sun block, which you would use every day in the summer but not the winter) you can't list it.
- In the right-hand column under each name and by each product, make a note of the most convenient place for

the person concerned to reach for each of those products, for example, if your daughter washes her hair with her fancy shampoo in the shower, it should go in there. If she washes it over the bath with the mixer tap, it should be by the mixer tap, or very close. Remember, human beings are lazy … sorry, creative!

- Note how many towels are in there and whether there is really room for them. If there isn't, you have a mess simply waiting to happen. Think about how you could accommodate having a place for everyone to hang up their towel neatly.

- List the 'ornaments' or accessories, if any, that you really, really love and that go well with the room. There should be no more than three including pictures. If you decide to include a set of candles, which counts as one item, they must match the bathroom and each other. (Okay, okay … if you like lots of visual stimulus you can add some more in later, but try sticking to three just for the moment to see what it feels like at the end of the exercise.)

- Think about the tasks that each of your family members use the bathroom for and when, and how that affects what is needed: for example, you will only need candles for baths at night, but if that's a favourite or regular habit with you, then they are essential. Visualising these will probably help.

This task should take you no more than 30 minutes and, eventually, you won't need to make lists, as you will automatically be thinking about this information in any room you are clearing. For the moment, however, it's useful to make this process of retraining your thinking more conscious by writing things down. If you notice that there aren't enough hooks for towels (i.e. there isn't one per person) or that you have absolutely no place to store things in the shower, then...

- List the things you will need to create the systems that match the way the bathroom is being used. Do you need an extra towel rail or more hooks? Do you need a wire shower tidy with a compartment for each person? Where do you store extra toilet rolls? List the simplest solution, make it easy to implement, and think about whether it will be easy to clean. Put it on your shopping list to get before you tackle Part 2. A friend of mine couldn't get her bathroom sorted out until she realised that she had a 'hairstyling' persona and had bought really sophisticated hairdressing products and scissors, etc., that needed a storage place. We discussed it and realised that the best solution was one of those neat little trolleys that hairdressers have, so that she could store everything she used for styling in one place. Then she could tuck it away in the bathroom and pull it out whenever she wanted it.

You don't have to fill your bathroom full of storage units or towel rails. Keep it simple and stick to what you really need. But remember, if there isn't a convenient matching location with the right equipment in it for each task, for example, drying off after a bath (for which you need a good place to put your wet towel) or possibly storing dirty clothes when you strip off for the shower at night (for which you need a suitable laundry basket), then this is where the pile-ups start to occur, and the frustration levels can rise. After all, at that point, the room isn't fulfilling its function by supporting you to accomplish whatever you need to get done in it, as easily as possible. Use your list now to see all tasks that the room is used for are listed and properly accommodated, to make sure this doesn't happen.

■ Part 2

1   Get your lists, your bucket of water (with a tiny bit of washing-up liquid in it), your cloth, your bin bags and your two (or more) storage crates and go into the bathroom. Working as quickly as you can, remove all the listed essential toiletries for each person, and your three accessories or treasured ornaments, wiping each one down as you go and putting them in the first plastic crate. Throw away anything that is empty or broken into a bin bag and decant half-used bottles of the same thing into each other, wherever practical. If you store some basic cleaning materials in the bathroom, they should go in this crate too. In the second crate, put anything that is a duplicate product that you (or whichever family member concerned) will *definitely* use, and which fulfils one of the same functions

as any item on the essentials list. So keep the extra and full bottle of your favourite shampoo that you bought, but this is not the time to hang on to that scented hand lotion Auntie Dora gave you two Christmases ago. The one that you haven't used because you never use hand lotion, but which you have kept because you think you should use it but never seem to get round to doing it. Of course, don't throw out any item that you think someone else would really miss, but consider putting it in the duplicates crate or back in their room. Or store it, and see if they miss it.

2   Relocate anything that shouldn't be in there, like the kids' slippers, to their proper rooms.

3   Remove towels, dirty clothes, etc., and put them in the laundry basket.

4   What is left, with the exception of the toilet brush, is clutter. For the next part of the exercise, don't allow yourself to take longer than 30 seconds to make a decision on any one item. Try pretending it's too hot to hold for long...

- Go through all the items and put as much as you can and anything you can't give away in a bin bag for rubbish, immediately.

- Make a pile of stuff that you *can* give away to someone else and leave it in another bag by the front door to do that, immediately, labelling it if you need to.

- Remove anything that you need in another part of the house and put it there immediately. This includes treasured ornaments that you can't part with but don't fit into your list of three for the bathroom. It also includes piles of clothes or other things that are not needed and will not be used in the bathroom. Put these in their appropriate rooms.

- A special note to parents. Bathrooms are not the place for your little darling's artwork ... the space is too humid. Put any pictures away in the kitchen for now. And limit the number of bath toys kept here. You can always rotate them.

  The bathroom should now be empty. If it isn't, *make a decision* on any remaining items and remove.

5 The next step is to deep clean the bathroom. My tip here is to spray all the surfaces with appropriate cleaners and go off and have a cup of tea. After all you have been working hard! Come back after 10 minutes, having left the cleaning products to start taking effect, and give the room a scrub. It is important not to get distracted at this stage. Don't let yourself take too long over this or it will be another form of procrastination. Put some music on and *get this done within an hour.*

6 Get the first crate and, using your list to help you, replace all the essential items *where they will be used.* This is crucial to the exercise. Remember that things must be located where they are easiest to use if you are going to

find them when you need them, and put them back auto-matically. If you have bought a shower tidy or an extra towel rail to facilitate this, now is the time to get it out and fit it. Group by task rather than by similarity. So if you have a beauty routine that you do straight out of the shower, for example, using talc, deodorant and mois-turiser, then group all the items for that routine together so that you are not having to search through other people's perfumes or aftershave, etc., to find yours. Obviously, with products for your shower routine of lathering up and washing your hair, all these products should live in the shower because that's where you use them. You don't need to put your talc or deodorant in there, because you can't use those whilst you are still wet. Group toiletries where appropriate for other members of the family too, not forgetting to put items for younger members within their reach.

7   If you have a new laundry basket or a new storage bin or chest of drawers, put it out now in the most conven-ient place for the task you had in mind.

8   Put out your fresh hand towels, bath mat and bath towels. Put the candles where they will be used to best effect. Put out your ornaments/mirrors, etc., using an artistic eye to do this.

9   Put all the cleaning materials away in the kitchen, except for the essentials, such as the cleaning fluid for

the toilet bowl. Leave the storage crate with the duplicates in the hall for the moment. You can put it back in the bathroom, or better still, in a cupboard for when it's needed, later.

10 This is a really, really important step, so take your time over it. Go into the bathroom and admire it! Luxuriate in the space, the order, the clean smell and harmonious colours. Congratulate yourself. You have done it! You have created this beautiful order out of chaos. This room is now designed to serve *you* properly. Store this image and feeling in your head... This is the equivalent to the 'reveal' moment in all those makeover shows.

11 The next step is an ongoing task and perhaps the most important step of all. Promise yourself that you will keep the bathroom like this for two weeks. See how it feels. Replace not just your toothbrush, but now your towel, your dirty clothes, your shampoo, etc., in the correct place first time, which is, after all, easier now that all of these items are more to hand. Don't put it down in the wrong place to come back to later. Don't bring anything new in that isn't absolutely essential right now. If you have to, make sure you place it straight in the correct 'zone' for the task. And, if other family members create piles of things in the wrong place, think about the pattern of use that would make them do that, and adjust the storage places if you can. Aim for it to be natural for everyone who uses the

bathroom to put things back in their correct places first time.

You are building new habits and making them more likely to stick, by backing them up with a physical system. The new arrangement of the bathroom makes it easier for you to be tidy but you must make putting things away correctly in there, first time, a rule. If you find that hard to do, go back to your 'reveal' moment and recapture the feeling that comes from that 'pristine' quality in your mind. You want to maintain this feeling. After two weeks you should be experiencing having one room in the house that is easy to use, quicker to clean and that seems to keep itself tidy with very little help, apart from the obvious changing of toilet rolls and towels and a once-a-week clean.

What have you achieved?

You may think that clearing out the clutter is the most important part of what you've done. Actually, creating and maintaining a system that keeps you clutter-free is the aim of the whole exercise. I don't know about you, but I don't want to be tidy if it means that I have to spend hours every weekend clearing and tidying. I want to *live* clutter-free, all the time, without too much effort.

Chapter three
Your vision

In this next section of four chapters, we will look first at what will motivate you. Then we will look at what is holding you back. And finally, how you can harness the habits and tendencies you already have, to help you create and maintain the order that you would like in your home.

Why and where do you want to be better organised?

You're not going to be better organised unless it is important to you. So this chapter is all about getting in touch with what is less than ideal for you in your home just now, and how you would like things to look. Take a moment right now to write down what you think clutter is. Then list all the places in your home that you think are cluttered, which hamper you, and which you would like to do something about.

Here is my definition:

Clutter is any thing that you don't feel good about or that stops you using your space in a way that either empowers or nurtures you.

Your emotions and the way you live are very closely linked, either in a positive or negative sense. One of the most common ways of stopping yourself achieving something that you really desire, but which actually challenges or scares you a little too much, is to make your space and time so disorganised that you don't create that thing in your life. That way you can let the chaos take up your headspace and stop you thinking about the fact that you are not achieving it. In this chapter we will be asking questions that help you to solve your emotional blocks to being organised and to harness the positive feelings that will help you get there.

Who do you want to be?

There is an old story about a rich man who wished to know to which of his three sons to leave his thriving business. He knew that the best thing was to leave the firm in its entirety to the cleverest son so that it was in the safest hands, and split his remaining accumulated fortune between the other two. In order to find out which son was the canniest, he decided to set each of them the same test. He called all of them together at sunrise and assigned each of them a large empty room in his house telling them that by the time the sun had set, each son must have filled his respective room as fully as possible with the most valuable thing he could find. The father gave each son five pieces of silver to help him in his task.

The eldest decided that he must use something naturally plentiful, so he decided to fill his room with rocks. All day he laboured until, by sunset, the room was full of rocks. When he had finished, he was very tired and dirty. The middle son decided to use something with a great deal of volume to fill the space, so he went out and bought many sacks of feathers and by midday he had emptied them out and had filled his room. Then he sat and thought about how unfair having a test was, and what a silly one his father had set. The youngest son, who was looked down on by the other two as a bit of a dreamer, sat and thought for a while ... in fact for most of the day, and then as the sun started to get low in the sky he disappeared into the marketplace. The other two watched him go, shaking their heads and laughing.

Sunset came and the father and three sons gathered together and went to each room in turn. The father saw the rocks in the eldest son's room and nodded. He saw the feathers in the middle son's room and nodded again. Then they made their way to the last room. The father pushed open the door. At first sight, the room seemed empty ... until the father noticed that there were a dozen lamps and all of them were lit. The youngest had filled his room with light. The father beamed with joy! This son had understood the task.

Which son would you rather be? Do you want to fill your rooms with things that are meaningful to you and that enhance your quality of life and enable you to work and to live in a better way? Or do you just want rooms that are full?

What could your clutter be hiding about you?

Your clutter can create a very effective physical barrier around you. It may be a way of shutting other people or questions out, and making you feel safer. If your fairy godmother appeared this minute and waved her wand and your clutter instantly disappeared, what other problems would you have to face? Take a minute to imagine that now…

- If your space was a haven for you and always clean and harmonious, what would you expect yourself to be able to do?
- What would others expect you to do?
- If you imagine yourself setting off on that particular journey, what are you most afraid of? Why?
- If your clutter makes you feel safer, can you create that feeling of safety in a less inconvenient and more effective form?
- On the other hand, if you were clutter-free, would others start expecting all sorts of things from you that you don't want to provide?
- Can you find another way of tackling any of this more directly?

Try asking yourself these questions now and writing down the answers as honestly as you can. There may be something that is getting in your way or not. Obviously, the ideal thing to do is to tackle whatever issues are stopping you. You may decide it's really important to do this first and put this book down for a while. But there is another way, if you want to keep going with the clutter clearing. You don't have to do it all at once. A good step is to acknowledge to yourself what you may have to face, or want to do, and why you may find that scary. Then, and this is the important thing, *separate* it from the question of being organised. Just because your life becomes more efficient doesn't mean that you *have* to work on this other issue, right now. You can enjoy a nicer space without it meaning that you have to solve all your other problems at the same time. It is hard to let go of a habit that, however illogically, makes you feel safe, but it is well worth doing. You are actually making life harder for yourself by creating chaos. If you are able to let go of it you may find that you are actually up to the task of sorting out your other issues.

You can put the knowledge that you have just gained about yourself on to the back burner for the moment, and get on with clearing clutter if you have been able to separate the two. Or you can always go back to it, in your own time, and decide either:

- Not to go for that goal or expectation and scare yourself any longer.
- To let your subconscious mind come up with an answer, by mulling it over before you go to sleep and then letting it go for a while, to see if any ideas occur to you.

- To focus on a way of tackling your fear and taking one significant step towards overcoming it. You can do this as an entirely separate thing, right now. That way, you can deal with the issue at the same time as clearing out your physical space.

If you find you have a real and difficult issue to deal with, be compassionate with yourself, and get the best help that you can. If necessary, put some time and effort into finding a good therapist and deal with your problems directly.

Some of you will put this book down right here. I'd guess that those of you that do will have realised that your clutter is important to you. You will have realised that your clutter actually does serve a very real purpose in your life, and that you don't wish to change that fact, just at the moment. If you decide not to change for this reason, then you will have saved yourself a lot of time. The rest of you will have decided, either that you wish to face what you are scared of, or that you wish to stop letting that particular issue interfere with the process of living more enjoyably in your own home – or both.

What is the point of being organised and clutter-free?

Being organised and clutter-free is not an end in itself. We were none of us designed to be perfect and 'static'. When

I was little I used to think that I wanted our house to be tidy and well coordinated because it was 'posh' and impressive. I don't know what I imagined myself doing within that imaginary 'perfect' picture, but it wasn't *living!*

Anyone who has ever spent a day modelling will tell you that lying around looking perfect is both tiresome and tiring. Sometimes the 'crash diet' approach to clutter clearing (i.e. do it as fast as possible to gain the greatest visual impact and to feel that you are finally 'tidy') fails, because getting to 'tidy' is the only goal. What happens over time? And why is looking tidy so important? Personally, I don't think looking tidy for its own sake *is* that important (although as it makes me feel more peaceful in my own home, my home does tend to look tidy most of the time). Having a space that supports you to do what you need to do with ease is important. But notice that there is another implication in that last sentence. It implies that once you are organised that you must actually get on with the *real* tasks (whether for work or pleasure) in your home. Making a list or clearing a table top can feel like an achievement (and so it is) but what is far more important in the long term is getting on with the significant tasks on that list or using the table to have a family dinner, etc. Clearing and organising are not ends in themselves. They are only useful steps to help you to get to your important goals. Please don't exhaust yourself with organising and neglect the important things in your life.

Your tidiness style

Take a moment to think about what your own tidiness style is. Do you like lots of 'visual noise'? Things that remind you of your loved ones or your good times? Think about this question carefully. I am asking you what makes you feel most at home. Of course, all of us will keep things that fall into these two categories, but do you need lots of these things on display to make you feel good? Do you like lots of ornaments and furniture, or plenty of space and clean surfaces? Which scenario feels most peaceful to you? If you like lots of visual interest around you, and need that to be happy, I am not trying to change you. What I am asking is for you to consider whether you have neglected to update the way things are organised so that they trip you up. Sometimes familiar clutter can be so comforting that, over time, more grows around it and makes life harder than it needs to be. Much of this book is written for those who want to achieve a minimalist look out of utter chaos, but don't know how. If that doesn't apply to you, remember that you can still benefit from the advice by making sure that your possessions are truly wanted, easier to find, up to date and easier to use.

Now let's get on with some more practical thinking about your space. What trips you up in your house? Is your kitchen or study hard to work in? Has it stopped you taking care of things or people in the way that you would like to? Is your living room too chaotic to relax in? Is your bedroom too busy to sleep in? Do you go on holiday to get away from your stuff or do you heave a sigh of relief when you close the door on it? Are you always losing things? What do you think your home says about you and what would you like it to say? How would you like to use the space you have, in a way that you don't, currently?

Visualising exercise

All you will need for this exercise is a pen and paper and about 45 minutes of quiet, uninterrupted time.

- Start to list the problem areas in your home that you would like to change and the frustrations these are causing for you at the moment. Include knock-on problems such as lack of time, irritation, or procrastination, as a result of the way these spaces hamper you. Write these down now.

- Then take the time to close your eyes and think about how you would like these areas to work and to look. Think about the practical benefits you would derive if they did flow more smoothly, and also write these down.

- Put yourself in this positive picture and ask yourself how you feel. Start to name these emotions, both positive and negative. Write down the positive and negative thoughts and feelings on separate lists. We will use the negative list in the next chapter, but for the moment, concentrate on the positive one. What have you written? Does the thought of things flowing more freely in your space make you feel more energised or calm? Or possibly more valued or nurtured? Try to dwell on the image or images that create these positive feelings and to remember them. We will be using them as we move on to more practical tasks.

• List the ways (if any) in which you would like to use your space differently, such as changing rooms around, or opening up the garden. These are your advanced projects, and we will look at these later.

Developing your visual sense

Some people are carrot orientated and some are stick orientated. The 'sticks' are in the next chapter when we look at some of the disadvantages of allowing your clutter to take over, but for now I am going to be talking to those of you who like 'carrots'.

One of the problems with being organised for some people is that they simply don't see their space in any other way from the way it looks now. The following exercise is to develop your visual sense. You will need to use that sense throughout this book to create a pull towards the completion of whatever you are clearing and to make the habit of 'completion' easier for you to maintain.

Scrapbook exercise

This is an optional exercise and can be done over time as you think more about your space. If you don't have the time to do it just now, or have more pressing clutter problems, then keep reading, but doing it really will benefit you.

Interior designers often use what is known as a 'mood board' when designing a room and explaining the feel that they are trying to create, to a client. This will include fabrics for major items such as chairs or curtains, the general colour scheme, and pictures that help to evoke the general style and feel of the room.

For this next exercise, I would like you to get yourself a cheap scrapbook and start to fill it with pictures of interiors or landscapes that inspire you. The landscapes may remind you of colours, textures, smells and a 'feel' that you relate to. Do you love the sea? Would you like a pale wood floor and light blue sofas in your sitting room to remind you of that? Do pictures of the city skyline at night remind you of the 'richness' you crave in your interiors? It is time to get back in touch with what pleases you visually.

You don't have to buy lots of expensive interior design magazines if you don't want to. You can beg some from friends or possibly ask for old ones from the overflowing pile in your doctor's surgery as they don't have to be too current. If you have access to the internet you can do some image searches online and print out the ones that you like to go in your scrapbook. You are going to cut the pictures that please you out of the old magazines, even if you don't know why they do, and paste them into your book. Doing that will get you looking at what goes with what, and how to fit your clippings into the pages. It may get you to see for yourself how important the empty space is between the pictures so that they look appealing.

As you do this, start thinking about styles you have always liked or hated. And consider what sorts of style would suit your current home and whether you have been honouring this. Think also about the level of visual interest you like in your home and how you want to create this. Do you want lots of pictures and ornaments? Or everything to be put away and every surface clean? Keep coming back to this process for a few weeks as your sense of your own taste develops, even if you are working your way very fast through the other exercises. It may eventually inspire you to decorate or freshen up your rooms with some new accessories and make it a more pleasant place. One that truly reflects who you are.

Your secret wish for 'flow'

Have you ever stayed in a really luxurious hotel room? One where everything was plush and coordinated, comfortable, tasteful, light and spacious? Did you find yourself taking a deep breath and sighing with delight? Most of us, however much we protest that we just love our clutter, will choose a luxurious and well-ordered hotel room over a cluttered one. Doesn't that mean that we all actually value the space and the flow in the room, i.e. the way in which everything is arranged to enhance your experience of using the room?

Detective exercise

Start paying attention to how you feel in various spaces. How do you feel when you are in a close friend's house if it is chaotic and cluttered? Panicked? Unwelcome? Cosy? If the feeling was negative, try to think about why that was... Did you feel unwelcome because there was no clear space for you to sit? Did it feel chaotic, because arranging even the simplest thing was difficult? Did you feel cosy because, although the sofa was piled high with washing, it was all clean and folded and sweet smelling rather than mixed up with everything else? How do the minimalist reception areas of office buildings or hotels feel? Flat? Clinical? Impoverished? Peaceful? Beautiful? Elegant? Do some detective work about what you like and why.

Got your vision now?

Okay, so perhaps now you have worked out what you would really like in your home. The way you would like it to look, feel, smell, etc. It is likely that you knew this at some level, all along. All of us have walked into either a private house or a hotel that we secretly wished we lived in full time... So what has stopped you creating that feel? 'Money! Time!' I hear you cry... Well, if you want to live in a Chateau in France and not the centre of Birmingham, and can't afford to move, I do understand. But it is likely that you could have created much more of the feel of what you truly love in a living space than you have taken the time to do in your own home. Why is that? It may be that you don't know how. Or it may be that every time you get near to trying, or even thinking about trying, all your resistances come up. So what is it that's stopping you?

Chapter four

So what's stopping you?

Your resistances

To start with, get out your list of negative feelings from the visualising exercise in Chapter 3 and look at it. Try to bear in mind what it says, as you read the following excuses, and work out which of these may apply to your current thinking:

'I know where everything is even though things look a mess'

This is usually the first reason people give for maintaining a cluttered space and the biggest reason people hang on to their chaos. It actually translates as: 'I'm afraid that if I put things away, I will lose them.' I used to rely on this system. In fact, it involves a useful element that I still utilise but in a more selective and effective way now. This system of yours relies on visual reminders that you use to prompt your memory. And once you start relying on visual prompts they are very hard to let go of, but if that's your only method of tracking things, you'll already know that visual reminders alone aren't very efficient.

You may think you know where everything is – half the time you do. But having huge piles of clutter on every surface and on the floor is a big price to pay because you're afraid that if you put things in cupboards you'll lose track of them.

This method also loses its effectiveness over time. There are two reasons for this: the first is that the eye starts to ignore what is familiar. Think about when we lived in caves, forests and savannahs. There were plenty of creatures that might have attacked us, and we needed to track animals for food. If we had been sensitive to every leaf, bit of bark or tendril of vine, we would have missed the vital clues that kept our ancestors safe and fed. We are not sensitive to every leaf in a section of forest that we know well. What we tend to notice is what has changed. This is so that we spot things like fresh tracks. So, back to your reminder system. What happens when a pile of things has been there for longer than a couple of days? You've guessed it. You don't really 'see' it any more. And the longer that goes on, the more that is the case.

The other thing that happens is this. Do you ever feel out of control with your clutter? As though your head is full of information that you are afraid you will forget? Do you feel tense? The brain has a short-term working memory and a long-term memory. Things that you wish to retain for long periods, such as the formula for the area of a triangle for instance, have to be repeated over and over in order to transfer them from the short-term memory to the long-term one.

The short-term memory can hold up to seven random items at one time – no more. Those people who remember the sequence of a shuffled pack of cards are doing just that … sequencing them. They chain the cards together in their memory using the techniques they have at their disposal. Therefore, they are only really memorising one item, which is the card that starts the sequence. Once this first card is remembered, all the others in the chain are recalled in order because their brain has linked them together, just in the way that you do with the separate digits of a phone number, or the words in the chorus of your favourite song. I call this 'bundling' and we will use it later on to help you to develop new habits.

Now when you try to remember the jobs that you have to do and where everything is in huge random piles of stuff, you are using a combination of short- and long-term memory to do this. But the point is that your short-term memory is constantly being overloaded, and that is what makes you feel so out of control and so tense. And the bad news is that as you get older this short-term memory can shrink. I can't remember seven items any more, in fact I struggle with more than four.

You shouldn't have to use your short-term memory to remember where things are. That is not what it was designed for. Using the toothbrush principle will make it very unlikely that you will 'lose' what you need to have at your disposal or forget what you need to do. Ever.

You will become much more likely to find what you need first time.

'If I put it away I'll lose it'

If you put an item away in the place that is closest to where you use it, not only will you be less likely to forget where you put it (because the place where you have stored it is no longer 'illogical' or 'random') but you will also be far more likely to use it and to replace it every time. Sometimes, this means making a new storage arrangement especially for it. I have a terrible memory; perhaps you do too. The only things that act as visual reminders in my home are things like letters to post on the hall table that are only there for a short period, i.e. until I next go out. Everything else gets put away. I hardly ever lose anything. I haven't lost anything in the house for over three years. (Gloves dropped in the street are another matter...)

'I can't throw that out, I may need it sometime'

I will confess here that about once a year I discover that I have thrown out some item, which, if I had kept it, I could have found useful. Yes, this costs me money, as sometimes I have to replace it. However, that is once a year or so, when I have made literally thousands of decisions not to keep something or not to allow it into my space in the first place. One wrong decision in, let's say, a thousand. That's not a bad margin of error.

Now let's look at the other side. How many times have you said, 'Ah, I have just the thing for that...' and taken half a day to find the thing, only to discover when you do (*if* you find it!) that it isn't as suitable as you thought, or even worse, it is damaged or too dirty to use because of the way it has been stored? And beyond that, how many times have you simply forgotten that you had it, gone out and bought a new one, only to come across the old one that you had stored, some months later? In the meantime, your everyday tasks are hampered by a state of chaos so that you can never be accused of being 'wasteful'. Does that sound worth it? Before you throw things out, we will use a system to discover if they are likely to be useful to you. It isn't foolproof, but it is good enough.

There is another reason people hang on to things in this category. You, like all human beings, like to believe you have unlimited time. Life would be unbearable if you didn't. So in your mind's eye you see yourself making your own jam or rebuilding your bike, or growing vegetables with the children or making your own Christmas cards. You have these cherished fantasies that live fondly and dripping with golden light in your imagination and you hang on to those old jam jars or tools, or old seeds or bits of wrapping paper, etc., so that you can maintain a connection with your dream.

But can you see that this is actually a deferred decision? You have deferred the decision either to put some time aside to grow the seeds with your children (before they turn 40!), or to decide that when Christmas comes, you'd rather spend the limited time you have planning a really lovely dinner or a party, than covered in glue and pretending that you love to be 'artistic' (assuming you don't really ... if you did, you'd already have put time aside to make the cards just for the fun of it, wouldn't you?)

It is hard to accept, but you only have limited time. There are only so many weekends in the summer that are going to be sunny even in a really good year. When I first heard a friend of mine acknowledging that and ruthlessly planning her social diary for the summer season, I felt really sad. I'd like to believe that summers are endless, the way they felt when I was a child and I couldn't tell the time. They aren't. And I'm not going to spend them making jam.

So the question to ask yourself, when faced with things that fall into this category is, do I really have the time to do that thing? Do I really enjoy it and is it a priority given everything else that I absolutely have to do? And if so, can I put a time in my diary when I can indulge my beloved jam-making habit (for instance) and actually do it? That is really important. Or am I going to be realistic and admit that I am probably never going to get round to it and throw that stuff out?

The almost foolproof system for knowing what you can let go of with confidence is this. You ask yourself if you are really going to use the item in question? And when? If you haven't got round to doing that thing in the last year I would guess you're not going to. If you haven't used that widget or piece of clothing in the last year, I would guess you're not going to. There are obvious exceptions, like skiing gear, for example, if you usually go skiing but haven't been able to afford it in a while. You know what these exceptions are. If, however, there isn't a definite occasion on which you are likely to use an item (in which case don't forget to move it to the best location for this) you probably won't.

If you really can't bear to part with some things, you can try putting it all in a (hopefully small) box and mark a date on it a year hence and store it out of the way. If you haven't taken the item or items out of that box in the meantime, you take the box down on that date and throw it away *unopened*. I don't really like this method because it doesn't help you to make decisions as you go and have faith in yourself that you can make the right ones but you can use it if you really have to.

'I hate throwing things away'

The source of this one is either an environmental conscience or a scarcity fear.

Some people do hate contributing to huge and over-flowing landfills. But there are far more environmentally friendly ways of dealing with your waste than letting it take over your house. For a start if you have useful items, you can recycle them so that other people don't contribute to global warming by buying new items that they could have got from you. If you have to throw things away because they are beyond their usefulness then recycle food, tins, clothes, shoes, glass, card, plastic, paper, etc. If you create the room in your house to sort and regularly give these items away, instead of letting them be hoarded, damaged and lost in your house, then you really will be doing something to help others and the environment. You may also buy less, because you use what you actually have. You may travel less because you are better able to relax properly at home. If you really want to help the environment then let things, such as the recycling and things you no longer need, flow through your house more efficiently, so that they can be used again by someone else. The other reason people hate throwing things away is a fear that nothing else will come in. This is also the reason people say yes to jobs and to relationships that don't really fulfil them. They are afraid that if they say no, that there won't be anything better and that they will end up with nothing at all. Be brave! Hold out for what you really want. Hold out for the thing that makes you feel great! Unfortunately, there is no way around this fear other than facing it.

This issue is really about quality rather than quantity. When you say no to something that is not right for you (however expensive...) you are saying that it isn't something that makes you feel great and therefore that it's not an item of quality for you i.e. it doesn't improve the quality of your life. You are subconsciously setting a bench mark for yourself. You are saying something to yourself about what you want and what you will accept in life and what you think you deserve.

Are you telling yourself at the moment, that any old junk will do for you? That living in a mess is okay because you can put up with it? Is that how you would want others to treat you? If you went to a birthday party and someone served you a piece of cake that had disintegrated, and they put that mess on your plate and pristine pieces of cake on everyone else's, how would you feel? After all it is still cake and still edible... Annoyed? But isn't that what you are doing to yourself? *And* isn't it how you are teaching others and life itself to regard you?

Every choice we make makes a series of others more or less likely. If I only have black clothes in my wardrobe and then I buy a pair of blue trousers, it is far more likely that I will want to buy other blue items to go with it. If blue doesn't really suit me, then that is a waste of time and money, even if the item was really cheap or given to me. And what is worse, whilst I am busy spending my money on blue tops to make that pair of trousers look good, I may miss out on some other bargain that would really have suited me. This is one of the pitfalls of keeping what isn't right for you even if it seemed thrifty to do it at the time.

This principle works on lots of levels. Remember Elizabeth Bennet in *Pride and Prejudice*? She had every reason to accept the awful Mr Collins. She had parental pressure from her mother, she was poor, with lowly connections and no dowry and was therefore unlikely to receive many offers. Marrying Mr Collins would have made it impossible for him to throw her family out of their house when her father died, so it was a means to save her mother and all her sisters from homelessness. And this was 150 years before the inception of the welfare state. She already knew that her favourite, Mr Wickham, was too poor to be able to marry her and that he would have to marry for money. She could have bowed to the pressure and 'settled'. She could have made everybody but herself happy and had their praise for her 'prudence' instead of their disapproval for her 'selfishness'. But she didn't. And because she dared to leave the space for something better in her life, in the end she married a good man whom she really loved and was rich to boot.

Yes, I know that is fiction ... but it works in real life too. If the space for the thing you really want is full of something not quite right, when it does comes along, it will go away again. That is to say, you won't be able to take advantage of the opportunity. If Elizabeth Bennet had married Mr Collins, Mr Darcy would have forgotten her and married Miss Bingley. And anyway, would you have admired her as much if she'd married Mr Collins?

Try taking a risk with something small like your clutter to test this out. If you sell some things, or make space to rent one of your rooms out, you may find you raise enough cash to buy what you really want, rather than putting up with second best. Or you may find that the right thing just turns up.

'I can't throw that away because it has sentimental value'

There are some things that are irreplaceable, have no practical use and are of no commercial value. Your child's first homemade birthday card to you, for instance, or treasured photos, or letters from your long-deceased grandfather. Of course if such things bring you joy, you should keep them.

But only if they bring you joy. If they carry a sad memory then, for the sake of your own happiness, I would ask you to consider letting them go.

Do you really want to keep those love letters from an ex-boyfriend or girlfriend? You run the risk of coming across them and feeling all that sadness again. Nothing is clutter if it brings you joy and enhances your life, whether it would be of value to anyone else or not. My guess is that you have items that fall into both categories, and only you can make the brave decision to let go of the ones that make you feel sad.

The next question is, can you find your sentimental items in order to enjoy them properly and are they well stored and safe from damage? The trouble with sentimental items is that they are often not used or enjoyed. Your father's medals ... perhaps you would enjoy them more if they were framed and displayed? Are your treasured photos in albums or are they all shoved haphazardly with the ones that didn't come out so well in a shoebox under your boots in the wardrobe? You are not as likely to get them out and look at them there, unless you are tidying up, and with any luck you will be doing less of that.

If you are not ready to let go, what you can also do is have an 'issues' box. Somewhere where you put things immediately that make you feel sad, but which you can't bring yourself to throw away. That way, when you are feeling brave, you can decide to tackle them. Doing this will mean that your pace and energy don't have to drop if you come across something emotionally painful, because you know where to put it for now. It will enable you to keep going with your clearing out and will stop you avoiding certain corners as well.

Not wanting to face the painful associations of some of your possessions is one of the chief reasons to let them build up. Be gentle with yourself here and do a little at a time. Clearing clutter that evokes an emotional response is both demanding and exhausting. Be brave and make a start. You'll feel so much better when it's done.

'I can't get rid of that dress/pair of shoes/handbag even though I don't really like it and hardly ever wear it, because it was soooooo expensive'

We've all done this. Gone shopping in an optimistic mood and spent a fortune on something hideous. And then we feel terribly guilty and really can't bear to admit it, so we kid ourselves we will use it some time and we get stuck. Fortunately, there are second-hand designer shops now where you can go and sell your guilty purchases, but only if you do something first... Forgive yourself. You made a mistake, but it was your money, or at least no one went without something because you spent it, if it wasn't. You aren't a child any longer. You are allowed to try out expensive hobbies that need lots of equipment and then decide they are not for you. It's your money. You are a grown-up now and you are allowed to make expensive mistakes occasionally. Or if you like, frequently.

If you own a sophisticated machine of some kind, you probably allow for a 5 per cent margin of error in the way it operates. You expect it to go wrong, and to need possibly expensive repairs. Everyone who owns a computer or a car will be nodding here, no doubt. Why aren't *you* allowed a 5 per cent margin of error? You're more valuable and sophisticated than your computer, and making mistakes and trying things out is the means by which you grow.

With clothes, I expect myself to make one really expensive and useless purchase every year. When I first started taking clothes seriously, the rate was much higher; something like 20 per cent of everything I bought. This is because I was learning about what really suited me, and I forgave myself and threw out the things I found I didn't like (or gave them to delighted friends) and accepted what I'd spent as a training expense. I needed to make mistakes to develop my eye for clothes. It felt like an investment in my learning. And these days I get lots of compliments on always being well turned out in any situation.

Forgive yourself and allow yourself to clear out everything that you don't like or that doesn't suit you. That item may be far better used and loved by someone else, or recycled. If you find it hard to do that, think about how you're going to feel if you sit in your own home surrounded by examples of your errors of judgement. Is that going to make you feel energised and motivated when you are learning or trying something new? If you are afraid that if you throw out what doesn't suit you, you will find you have nothing very much left, I'm afraid that is what you already have. Hiding that fact, by adding in lots of clothes that aren't useful, isn't going to change that. What's the worst that could happen? That you might have to go shopping? There are some ways to make your clothes shopping much more effective, which are listed in the Wardrobe section in the chapter on bedrooms (see pages 109–121), for those of you who are nervous shoppers. For the rest of you, well, being 'forced' to do the kind of clothes shopping you adore is just a sacrifice you'll have to make....

'That item doesn't fit me now, but it will when I've lost another 10 lb so I'll keep it for now'

Ah! Do you really want to be reminded, every time you open your wardrobe, that you are 10 lbs (4.5 kg) too big? What message does that send about you to your subconscious mind? What about first thing in the morning when you are deciding what to wear to work or for lunch with a friend? Do you think having five or ten items that don't fit, or are in need of repair, mixed in with the clothes that do, helps you to decide what to wear and helps you to feel confident in your choices? If your weight really fluctuates a lot and you have some wonderful clothes in a size either too large or small that you don't want to alter, then at least store them away in a box somewhere safely and don't get them out until they fit properly. Remember, that unless you are definitely going to lose 10 lb in the next year *and keep it off*, these clothes will go out of fashion anyway. Do yourself a favour and give them away or sell them.

Give yourself permission to celebrate losing that extra weight with some new purchases.

'I was given/inherited that. I would feel terrible about getting rid of it, even though I don't like it'

You were given it. It's yours. You own it. You can do what you like with it. If someone gave you an item that didn't fit you, they wouldn't complain if you changed it for the appropriate size. They would want you to use it and to enjoy it. Do you want to keep something that you don't like even though you feel guilty for hating it, and be reminded of that all the time?

Our parents played a very subtle game with us, concerning the ownership of things. They provided for us but kept an eye on what they had given us. This came home to me when I was seven because there was a programme on TV called *Swap Shop*. Children used to meet and swap games or dolls or toys and swapping became quite a craze at school. I asked my Mum if I could swap something and she said 'No'. I realised then that if she could stop me swapping it, it was because she still owned the item. She hadn't given it to me at all. She had just bought it and let me use it. It was still hers.

If you've inherited a valuable item or a piece of family history, talk to the person concerned if they're still around or anyone who would be affected by its sale. Other than that, anyone who wants to see you use what they have given you, as if they still have a stake in it, probably doesn't have your happiness in mind. Don't let them get away with that.

'I am lazy'

Yes, you are and so am I. If you object to being called lazy, I would offer another definition of laziness. Your subconscious mind keeps tabs on what is really important to you. Not what you say is important, but what is actually important. If there are things that you never get around to doing that you think you ought to, that is because there is still some level of conflict attached to doing them that you haven't been able to get over, just yet. My point is this. You eat and sleep because you enjoy it. You find time to exercise, or smoke, or have a cup of tea and a biscuit, or write in your diary, or watch your favourite TV show, or see your boy/girlfriend, and will rearrange your work and life around these habits, regardless of how busy you get. In fact, you will skive off other tasks in order to be able to do these things. That may seem like a very inconvenient fact of life to you when your accounts are still waiting to be done and you are being threatened with a fine, but it is actually a really good thing. It means that you never lose touch with what brings you pleasure and that is the most basic and important factor in your life. After all if you don't enjoy it, day to day, then what is the point of living? So that you can say you have accomplished a huge list of tasks that others thought you 'should' do?

The point of clearing clutter is not to look good or to have 'finished it'. It is to make it easier for you to spend time on the things you love to do. If you weren't 'lazy', i.e. not focused on this tiresome tidying up stuff but on what you want to do, there really wouldn't be any point in being well organised other than to make your house look as though a photographer was about to visit it. I can't think of anything worse... The reason, I would guess, that you haven't been tidy up to now is that you haven't had a time-efficient way of *getting and staying* organised. So you've refused to do it. Well done you!

'I resent spending time keeping my house clean and tidy and all the tasks I have to do, especially when I am tired'

Either you really are overworked and overtired (in which case you need to address these issues) or this is actually rebellion and resentment over having to be in charge of your life, and take care of yourself. No one can make your life run better but you. If you want to drift along and let things happen as they will, then that's okay. But take a little time to think about the benefits of having a system that keeps your life running fairly smoothly and helps you create time and space for what is important to you. Think about the extra power it would give you to actually create what you want most in your life, rather than simply making do with what life dishes out to you. You do actually have that power, even if you never learn how to use it. However, it will take a bit of thought and effort and some facing up to your fears to be in charge of your own destiny. Only you can decide if you think it's worth it.

'I haven't moved on'

Are you still living as you did when you were a student? Or as you did when your children were at home? Are you so attached to this period of your life, and who it made you, that you wish it still existed and you hadn't had to move on? Look at how you'd like your space to feel and to serve you now... And think about other ways to recapture the 'good old days' that actually suit you better.

'I collect things'

Ask yourself some questions about your collecting habit. How does your collection make you feel? What purpose does it fulfil in your life? Is your collection well displayed and stored and do you still get genuine pleasure from it? How much have you spent on it to date? Are you happy to continue to spend that much to collect, maintain, store and display it? Is it stopping you using rooms in your house the way they were intended to be used? Does your collection help you to define who you are, and are you afraid that if you got rid of it, you would lack any unique qualities? Sometimes, things change and you don't need to collect that particular thing any more... Only you can answer these questions and decide whether your collection is a life-enhancing thing, and brings you genuine joy, or whether it's time to let it go.

'Sticks'

Now let's look at things that you may miss out on if you don't clear your clutter. This is a section designed for those of you that find yourselves better motivated when you are moving away from the negative consequences of not doing something, than by understanding what you could gain. If you work better with positives, skip this section. It is important to remember, however, that some people don't.

'So what if my house is a bit or a lot messy? I am not really missing out on anything other than the accolade for being the world's most tidy householder am I?'

A house filled with clutter costs you time, and money, and more. Here's how:

- How long do you spend searching for items that you need – perhaps 30 seconds looking for the phone three times a day? A minute and a half a day. Ten and a half minutes a week. That adds up to just over 9 hours a year. Now factor in all the other things you spend extra time looking for.

- How long do you spend standing confused in front of your wardrobe or even trying things on, only to find that they need mending or don't fit? Perhaps 10 minutes a day? That's more than an hour a week. That's over two whole days a year. Factor this time in… Do you get paid less than you might because you don't look as professional as you could? It is said that you should dress for the job you want rather than the one you've got. Human beings are facile. This stuff really does make a difference. Factor in the money lost, too.

- How long do you spend moving items that are in the way to get to things you regularly need. Maybe one minute each time? Multiply it up by the number of incidents per day, week, and year... That's a *lot* of time.

- How much time do you spend procrastinating on what you have to do because even starting a job is really daunting when you have to fight to make space to get the job done and assemble the items you need? What could you be spending this time on if you managed your space better? Quality time with your partner? Planning for your dreams and making them happen?

- What are you able to avoid in your life because you have the excuse of the chaos around you and the struggle to keep up? Is that fair to the people around you?

- How often do you have to replace things because they get lost and damaged in your clutter? Can you really afford to throw that money away, even if it only amounts to £5 a week? (That's £260 per year, by the way.)

- I'm going to be really rude now. (People who know me personally won't be at all surprised...) How clean is your house? I'm guessing if your clutter problem is really bad that it is pretty neglected. Dust doesn't really matter, but the little creatures that love to live in it do. Do you know what dust is made up of? It's approximately 80 per cent dead skin cells. We shed them all the time. Leaving areas undisturbed to collect organic dust and dirt encourages some pretty nasty bacteria and vermin into your house. After all, you've left a free meal out for them. Yuck! And what about your kitchen and bathroom? One big clean a year or every few months in these two areas won't really solve your problem. You are cooking and eating and washing in both of them every day. Not paying attention here can make younger or older members of your family (who may not be as robust as you are) very ill. Do you want to do that to your family?

- Have you ever hesitated to invite someone to your house? Has the prospect of the clearing up you would have to do, or the way others might judge you if you didn't, overwhelmed you? Are you missing out on good times that you would otherwise have?

Time, money and health. Your connections to other people. Your dreams. Aren't these the important things in life? Shouldn't your home help you to get, or to keep them? If you have a partner, you may be pushing him or her away with all your 'stuff' and the chaos. If you have children the potential damage is even worse. Not only is it easier to make them ill, but they have no choice about the kind of environment they live in. They can't leave, or buy a night in a hotel to get away from the dirt and the mess!

The worst thing, though, is that you will be teaching them how to create mess in their own lives once they leave home (unless they rebel and learn how not to, for themselves). That isn't really fair is it?

Well, I've been hard on you. And perhaps you don't have any of these resistances, but your attempts to be more tidy and systematic have failed. Perhaps you have fallen foul of some of the more common myths about clutter...

Chapter five
Myths and bad habits

'I need to clear my clutter'...

This can actually be the biggest myth of all. Is clearing your clutter an excuse for not getting on with the work you actually need to do? Or would having a better system help you to get on with things? If you have a system that already works and you are looking to create perfection, ask yourself if this is a good use of your time... Compulsively clearing clutter can be a form of procrastination and a chronically bad habit. But if setting up a new system would help you to enjoy your house more, then read on.

'This house is too small'

This is very unlikely to be true. If there is a bedroom for everyone and a reasonable amount of storage space, what is far more likely is that you have decided to hang on to more things than are practical for you to have in your living space, and far more than you actually need. Assuming that you really have to store items for someone, or for reference, or for work, there is no reason why those items should be cluttering your living space. They should be stored somewhere else, even if you have to pay to do it. This is because if you worked out the proportion of your rent or mortgage that corresponds to the amount of space the things you're storing take up, you would find you are already paying several times what you would pay to have them professionally stored. Living space is expensive and it needs to be heated and lit. It doesn't make sense to use it to store lots of things. Anyway, is storage more important than you are?

When I was little, I got into terrible trouble if I broke anything even if it was very obviously an accident. It didn't matter how inexpensive the item was. If I broke it, I was shouted at. I was a very clumsy child and I got more and more nervous handling things, so this became a bit of a vicious circle. The message I got was that anything, however cheap or trivial, was more important than I was, and that 'things' were more important than I was. With an attitude like that, it was easy to believe that storing possessions in a way that hampered my living space was okay because they were more important than my convenience... But for you, isn't it time to put your own comfort first?

One of my friends grew up with the message that 'She who has the most toys, wins'. Naturally she was loath to get rid of anything. How about replacing that with 'She who has the *best* or "most loved" toys, wins'? It is quality of life that we are trying to improve for you here.

The only exception to this myth is if you are living in a very small place, perhaps a studio flat in an expensive city, or a room in a shared house, and have to make that one room fulfil all the functions of a house for you. If that is the case, I suggest that you read all the preliminary chapters here with the basic principles in them, and go to the chapter on living spaces for some extra tips on how to make a smaller living space work for you. If you have a problem with weeding your possessions ruthlessly, you'll find the chapter on storage spaces, which covers this in more detail, useful to skim through too.

'I've read lots of clutter-clearing books and most of them say that you have to commit to doing a proper tidy-up every day in order to stay organised'

Yes, they do tend to say that, don't they? Usually in the back of the book once you have slogged through the entire thing or even the entire process and feel you never want to think about your possessions ever again…! In fact, if you organise your home well in the first place and you commit to replacing things properly immediately, general tidying-up sessions are almost never needed.

'I need two of everything'

Why do you have duplicates of things that you won't give or throw away? Do you use them for two separate tasks in two locations? If that is the case, it is a legitimate reason. For instance, if you have a good pair of scissors in your office and a good pair with your sewing projects, that is fine. But two kettles? Two irons? Some people have two of everything because they want to double the chances of finding what they need! If you set this system up properly and use it you won't need to do that. If you inherited the duplicates (from your parents' home for instance) and hate throwing useful stuff away, see the point in the previous chapter about throwing things away.

'It's out of fashion now but I'll wear it again when it comes back round'

If the item of clothing is genuinely a designer article and beautifully made then, yes, it may be cherished in a vintage shop or a museum (eventually). If you're not going to wear such an item now then it should be stored somewhere safe, or sold. But most of your clothes aren't that special, are they? Yes, everything comes back in fashion but as an influence. The materials used, colours and cut are likely to be slightly different. Flares came back into fashion when I thought that they never would. But if I'd kept my purple velvet ones from 1976, even assuming that they would still fit me, I don't think I'd have worn them again…

'It isn't me that makes things messy, it's my partner or kids…'

I was helping someone to clear clutter recently that used this excuse. We looked around at the volume of junk and analysed it pile by pile. It was 85 per cent hers. Her partner did leave bits of paper around with notes on them to remind her to do things but we solved this by getting an in-tray and asking him to put them in there. Kids, for better or worse, follow your lead. They won't be tidy if they don't see you being systematically organised. The primary reason for this is that they don't know how, because you haven't taught them yet by example.

You are the one that has picked up this book and decided to read it. Your partner may like mess and may not want to change. That is who they are and if they are happy then I have no quarrel with that. There is a point at which you will need to get your partner or your kids involved if you want to be tidy in most areas of your home, most of the time, but don't make the mistake of thinking that your partner is the reason you can't start this process. Even if you do have a pathologically messy partner, there are probably some areas of the home that are your 'domain'. Your bedroom? Your wardrobe? The kitchen? A shed? The garage? Are these well organised? Start in these areas and lead by example. I strongly advise that you *say nothing*, learn the system yourself and let the benefits become obvious. Even if you don't make a convert of your partner you will still be further on than if you hadn't started. I would guess, though, that because you aren't being preachy or trying to change them they will be less resistant to the idea of trying out being better organised and may do so even before you mention it. I have seen this happen a few times. Please don't nag them, though. And on no account tidy up their stuff. Things can have some very personal emotional attachments and they will have every right to be furious with you if you do. Just start with your own work first.

With your children, I think it is perfectly reasonable to ask children of any age to tidy up their toys in communal areas at the end of the day if you have provided a place for them to do that, for example, a big toy chest in the living room. Teenagers with their own rooms have far too much pressure on them in general to make keeping their room tidy an important issue. Their hormones are going crazy and their brains are literally rebuilding and reorganising. Hygiene and cleanliness are important, for the obvious reasons, but other than that, their rooms are *their* space.

'I've got to keep that, I'm storing it for someone…'

Sometimes, it is a kind and pragmatic thing to do to store things for a friend or a relative, especially your children, if they are travelling for a year or about to move into a new place. If you have agreed to do this I would suggest that you find a way of storing the items that doesn't hamper you and cramp your living space and that you put a definite time limit on the arrangement and stick to it. There is no reason, once your children have left home, that they should regard your home as a dumping ground for their unmade decisions about their possessions, for indefinite periods. And if you are aiding and abetting them in this, why is that the case? Do you want to avoid being called selfish? Do you want to hang on to them in some way? Are you secretly hoping they'll come back to live at home again? It's your space. Use it in the best way to make you happy.

'I am messy by nature and I like my clutter'

If your clutter makes you feel good then I am not trying to persuade you to do anything differently. My definition of clutter is anything that hampers you or doesn't make you feel good. If you don't feel guilty or ashamed of the mess and you love your bohemian dinner parties where everyone sits on the floor by candlelight amid piles of books because the sofa is piled with stuff and the bookcases are over-flowing, and this makes you feel happy, that's just fine. Within that general state, though, is there anything you're not happy with? A certain room or task that is hard for you to work in or get through? Think about applying these principles to that area to see if it makes things any easier.

Be careful with this one, and be honest. Do you think your mess makes you look more 'creative' or 'interesting' or busy or in demand? Chances are that it doesn't influence people either way, and that they base their opinion of you on much more than that. The sad fact is that if you're not creative or bohemian or intellectual then no amount of objects or mess will make you seem so. There isn't a short cut. Anyone can hoard stuff or be messy! It isn't a special trait.

'I'm a "princess", I hate the idea of having to deal with all this'

One of my friends who claimed to be too spoilt to deal with her clutter turned out, upon more careful question-ing, to be anything but. She is a single mother, has three children, and works as an alternative health practitioner and teacher. She spends all day giving selflessly to others and had inherited much of her unwanted clutter from a parent, who perhaps should have thought far more carefully before passing it on. Underneath, she was feeling very resentful about this and we realised that she needed to create a little bit of self-nurturing time to start balancing her life. She also saw that if her house was less messy the space in itself might feel more supportive and nurturing to her at the end of a long day. She said she resented having to do this for herself, but if she doesn't do it at least a little, she will be teaching the world that it's not important to her, so the world won't rush to provide it for her.

'I just don't have time to be organised'

Do you have the time and money *not* to be well organised? If your clutter problems are really bad, I'd guess you already spend hours losing things and looking for them. I suspect that you lose precious time walking around your clutter and constantly tripping over it, not to mention the time it takes to have to move three items to get to the one you actually want to use. This may be the reason why you don't have any time. You are probably also spending money you don't need to on replacing items that get lost or damaged because they aren't well stored. Sorting things out now will save lots of time later.

'I'll do it later…'

The old adage is 'If you don't have time to do it right the first time, when are you going to have the time to do it over?' This is absolutely correct. When you defer the decision to do something, whether it be putting something away or starting on a project, you actually increase the amount of time that it is going to take for you to complete it. This is because your brain has to pick up the threads and remember where it was with the task when you put it down (a bit like the time your computer takes to boot up in the morning). It is much quicker to strike whilst the iron is hot. It's a myth that staying organised takes lots of time and that being slightly (or more than slightly) disorganised saves time. *Getting* organised does take time. I agree with you there. But if you do it properly, it hardly takes any time at all to stay that way.

'Doesn't everyone have to scramble around shamefacedly tidying away their mess if one of their friends says they're popping round?'

Ah ... no. Many people don't have to.

'One day I will have a really nice place and then I will be motivated to keep it tidy and well ordered.'

You could probably enjoy the space you have a lot more than you do, if you let yourself look after it a little more. And when you get to that dream house, if you haven't learned how to be orderly, do you think you will magically know how, when you are presented with the key? A house that could teach you that would be worth twice the price!

'If I have a big clear-out that will solve the problem'

Will it? If you clear things out but don't change your habits, won't you find things building up again? Clear-outs without a change of habits are, as I've said earlier, like crash diets – they only ever work in the short term.

'One day I am going to solve this by getting a cleaner'

So, how are you thinking this will work, exactly? If you hire a cleaner, are you going to tell them where everything goes and expect them to remember? Are you happy either to pay them to tidy up as well as clean, or for them to make little piles of your stuff so that they can at least try to get to the surface they are supposed to be cleaning? And have you thought about how much extra your cluttered surfaces will cost you to have cleaned? Imagine an empty kitchen counter. How long does it take to spray and wipe with a damp cloth? About five seconds? Now imagine it full of stuff such as blenders, jam jars, Post-it® notes, recycling, etc. How long does it take to spray and wipe it now? About 15 seconds? Now multiply that difference for every surface that is cluttered in the house and convert it into hard cash. Then multiply it by 52 to get the yearly cost. Actually it will take even longer than that. Cleaners are people too. They like to take pride in their work. Utter chaos and a place that hardly looks any different, even when they have finished cleaning, is going to slow them down even further, because cleaning your home feels like a thankless task and a struggle.

I have a cleaner. She has cleaned for me every week for 12 years now. She is not a particularly fussy person but if I so much as dirty a cup and leave it in the sink whilst she is with me, she will wash it up before she goes, even though I have never asked her to. That is because my kitchen (as well as the whole house) is pretty tidy and she enjoys taking that last look at a job well done before she leaves. I recommended her to a more untidy friend of mine. Big mistake. She cleaned for him once and vowed never to do it again as his vacuum cleaner broke down from the shock of being used and having to cope with the huge build-up of dust. A cleaner cannot take responsibility for something that is yours to sort out.

'I don't know how to stay organised. I tidy up but three days later things are a mess again'

This may well be true. You may know how to store things efficiently, but not in a way that facilitates their easy use. You need to use the system in the following chapters...

Other common traps and bad habits

Aside of these common myths, there are a few other points I would like to deal with here.

'I really want to buy this item even though I've no idea where I'll keep it'

Try to be disciplined when you acquire or buy things, large and small. If you don't know immediately where you will keep the item so that it will be convenient to use, you are likely to dump it somewhere and clutter up your space with it for some time to come, or even worse, forever! You will undo all your hard work if you don't take a moment each time to think about the best place for a new thing.

'Technology will speed me up'

Technology brings its own breakdowns and problems and lots more things to find space for. If you are not working well and efficiently now, having more equipment will only provide one more layer of mess and one more excuse for procrastination. It can be a great thing, but only if you use it well.

'I may as well tidy/clean/repaint/rebuild this other room whilst I'm here'

Falling into this trap comes out of the fear that you will never visit this cluttered corner again. If you distract yourself so that you don't complete the job in a reasonable amount of time, then you may get so fed up that this becomes true. So you are creating a self-fulfilling prophecy there. Do one thing at a time. Clear one area at a time. Get used to experiencing the completion of what you set out to do, before you are exhausted, and experience patting yourself on the back for it. Trust that you can establish a system that keeps you fairly clear, so that you can go back and repaint or whatever you want to do when you have the time, and that you will feel like doing it.

Things don't have to be done perfectly for them to

keep moving forward in the right way. Sometimes 'good enough' is all that's needed. It's often better to make a start than to defer doing anything for ever.

'You get far more done if you can multi-task'

This is true only in those circumstances where you would otherwise not be required to think about one of the tasks in hand. So if you set your washing machine or dishwasher going whilst you deal with your in-tray and only have to remember to empty it 40 minutes later, that is true. It is also true if you are on a train and are able to catch up on paperwork as you travel. But people are very rarely able to concentrate effectively on two things at once and even if you are, this capacity diminishes as you age. People in their twenties will continue to chatter as they walk a difficult rocky path but 60-year-olds will instinctively fall silent when they come to the tricky bits as their brains concentrate on the terrain ahead. The chances are that your multi-tasking is creating chaos around you because you're probably not actually completing tasks and putting the items that you've used away. If you're a Mum multi-tasking may be unavoidable, but try to go back to doing one thing at a time and completing it before you move on to the next one, when you can. It's much more satisfying, and makes staying tidy easier.

'If you work long hours you will get more done'

Your brain gets tired, and after a while it stops working at maximum efficiency, so you take twice as much time to get a simple task done. And if you get into that state you are far more likely to give up and either leave half-finished tasks around or let things become messy. It is far better to let yourself rest, and look into why you are routinely asking yourself to work long days in the first place. Working that hard isn't sustainable and it is better to work to live, not live to work. Sometimes, a proper break will enable you to come up with a neater solution to a problem whilst you rest. Let your brain help you by respecting its rhythms. The following trap goes hand in hand with this one…

'If you want something done, do it yourself'

This myth is a bit like the one that if you put anything down or away, then it will never get done. Delegate to other people by checking how much help you think the person you have delegated to will need, and schedule in regular checks with them so that you don't reach your deadline and suddenly find they have let you down. If you are using the systems I recommend in the first home office chapter (see pages 151–192), it should be easy to remember to do this. Give them your goal, and any essential parameters or rules, and let them use their own method. It can be liberating to realise that people are just as capable and intelligent as you are, even if they do things differently. Being overly busy and frazzled is not a sign that you are needed, important or loved. It is much nicer to have the time to feel these things properly and to enjoy feeling them instead.

The need to buy hope

If you find yourself helplessly buying and filling the house with things you never use, ask yourself if you are buying hope. The advertising industry constantly presents us with unrealistic standards to hold ourselves to, and then provides the 'solution' in the form of the product they are selling. We learn to think that we can 'buy' our way out of any problem and this becomes an insidious and habitual way of thinking. Obviously sometimes we can, but it does-n't tend to work very well with the important things in life. Your need to splurge in a particular area, such as clothes or make-up or books or cars or toys, may actually be a symptom of a deeper anxiety that you are not tack-ling head on. You may be using your purchases to make yourself feel better about the situation temporarily. Of course you have every right to do that if you so wish. But wouldn't it be better to find out what's bothering you and take some more positive steps to solve the problem of the way you feel? Then you could spend the money you save on something that you would really enjoy...

When I was a child, my mother was often impatient with my mistakes and kept telling me I was stupid. I didn't go to university and when I finally had money of my own I spent it on book after book. Many of them languished on my shelves unread because I didn't have time to read them all. And as I was reading them out of insecurity I didn't buy books I enjoyed either, but ones that would 'improve me'. Reading them felt like hard work and I felt constantly 'reproached' for my stupidity as I did so. Book shops made me feel disorientated and really quite upset. There seemed to be an endless stream of information in them that I couldn't possibly absorb.

I don't buy lots of books any more. I have worked out that I am not that stupid. And that sometimes it is okay to be stupid, and that I learn more if I just let myself 'be', until I have absorbed what I need to and what I am truly interested in. There will always be people that know far more than I do. When I meet them, I hope that the simple human warmth they receive from me will make them consider me still worth talking to, anyway.

Storing items for your fantasy selves…

I visit some people who actually store their possessions in a very orderly fashion, but whose high-traffic areas are chaos because all their storage spaces are full. This is a very common problem. It is all useful stuff that they may use some time. It is well stored and categorised, but there is far too much of it. They have an item for every occasion and eventuality, and whole categories of things for every activity in which they've ever been interested. On the face of it, it seems wasteful to throw all these possessions away but I think endlessly storing all these things, however neatly, actually comes out of a lack of perspective. Remember what your house is for. Is it for you to enjoy and live in joyfully? Or is it for you to store items that it feels like a crime to get rid of? There has to be room for *you*. And you are *BIG*. You need most of the space to do what you need to do and to feel nurtured.

The second aspect of this storing is the concept of carefully conserving items for other parts of ourselves that hardly ever see the light of day but whom we don't want to lose touch with, and thereby 'completing' ourselves with these possessions. This is the side of us that makes cards, or has an elaborate beauty routine, or strips engines or restores furniture or perhaps paints in oils. If you are running out of space, you can't afford to indulge this instinct any more. This is decision debt again. Make a decision about what you are really going to do/use in the next couple of years and let go of the rest. Let yourself shed that old skin from the person you once were. It isn't a loss, but a refining process. You are always becoming who you more truly are. If you need any more persuading, there is definitely a correlation between holding on to your older (or past) selves mentally, and having too much body fat!

Fear of empty space

Some people really do feel uncomfortable leaving clear spaces on their surfaces or on their desks. This may relate to a fear of going without or lacking things. A full space isn't necessarily full of things that actually enhance your life. If this is your issue and you are able to deal with it, well and good. Try weaning yourself on to leaving one square foot of space on your desk always clear. Then increase it to two. Then maybe the whole desk. What feelings come up for you? Note these and try to get to the root of the problem. If you can't, then try to cut back your stuff to the point where there are designated places to leave the 'active' items on, say your desk, or in your kitchen ... i.e. that there is empty space but you know that it is going to be filled with items you are going to use. That way, your active items won't be the ones that are always tripping you up. If you are studying, leave a space on a shelf that is the place that you always put your course homework when you come in. Then you don't have to tidy your desk before you can work.

The Japanese have the right idea, because they regard space as a 'thing' not the 'lack of a thing'. Space is some-thing that can be aesthetically pleasing, make a task simpler (this book would be much harder to read if I didn't leave a space between each word) and can be used in its own right. (If you don't believe me, try holding a party in a broom cupboard.) Empty space, where appropriate can be a 'thing' that you use and that enhances your life, not a 'lack' or a negative.

'I have a real problem. I can't stop spending/ acquiring/hoarding things. I can hardly see my living spaces properly, or use them any more. And the mad thing is, it's stuff I don't really use or enjoy. I am getting into debt, and yet I can't seem to stop...'

If this is you, it's great that you've admitted this to your-self. That is a very courageous thing to do. Facing your rising panic rather than ignoring it, and being aware of what's going on for you, is a huge first step. You probably need help that is specific to you and beyond the scope of a book. My best advice would be to get some counselling and try to work out, with the help of a therapist that you 'click' with, why you are being motivated to acquire things and what function that habit is fulfilling for you, so that you can deal with your need more effectively. This will make you much happier.

On the practical side, arrange to get some debt counselling if you need it. The 'Money Saving Expert' website run by Martin Lewis from *It Pays To Watch* on Channel 5 has a great page on this at http://www.moneysavingexpert.com/loans/debt-help-plan. If you can meet your minimum repayments, have a look at the strategies he suggests for getting the situation under control. If you can't make your minimum repayments, you are in debt crisis and you definitely need help. Ideally, you should try a non-profit debt counselling service that is available from the following places in the UK:

- Consumer Credit Counselling Service – Telephone: 0800 138 1111 Website: www.cccs.co.uk
- National Debtline – Telephone: 0808 808 4000 Website: www.nationaldebtline.co.uk
- Citizens Advice Bureau – Website: www.citizensadvice.org.uk or visit your local CAB centre
- Community Legal Advice – Telephone: 0845 345 4345 Website: www.communitylegaladvice.org.uk

If you can't face getting therapy, enlist the help of a friend (it's probably best not to make it a family member) to 'buddy' you whilst you start to clear your stuff and to help you with budgeting your finances. Make sure it is someone sensible and reliable, and schedule regular appointments and assessments with this person. Set yourself a realistic goal so that you can look back and congratulate and reward yourself as you achieve your goals.

If your hoarding or spending is causing you a problem, remember that it doesn't have to be like this. Please make sure you get the help you need. You *can* slowly get yourself back on track and you'll be so glad you did.

Have you run out of excuses yet? Good! Now let's look at how we can use the instincts you already have to create some good habits that will stick.

Chapter six
Getting started with good habits

The 'lint' instinct

Have you ever seen someone who is immaculately dressed, except that they have somehow picked up a piece of thread or lint on their jacket? Didn't you just itch to pick it off? They were only one simple step away from perfection (or in our terms 'completion') and you wanted to complete the process as a result. Town councils have found that if they do things like mend broken windows and clean graffiti up, it has a good general effect on the rate of vandalism and petty crime even in a tough city like New York. This is because taking care of your immediate environment sends a good message to the subconscious mind about the standard expected, and the level of care. If everything is clean and put away in its proper place in your kitchen, you are far less likely to tolerate a wrapper and crumbs on the counter. You are far more likely to clean up as you go. You are programmed to 'complete' but you may have created so much visual clutter that you have stifled this good instinct in yourself. I'd like to help you to resurrect and reinforce it in yourself now.

Strengthening the instinct to 'complete' is what many of those exercises in Chapter 3, the 'vision' chapter, were about. If you have a finished picture in your mind's eye and feel inspired and enthusiastic about that picture when you start a project, you are much more likely to be 'pulled' or compelled to complete it. Look at those positive lists you wrote, again now. Remember the picture in your head and think about recreating it. Ideally, as you go through this book, you will constantly be comparing your current state of tidiness to the finished picture in your head and feel that you want to get there. This finished picture is also what is subconsciously in your mind when you see a surface that is tidy, but for one item. You know what it 'should' look like and want to recreate that. Try to keep calling your ideal images up regularly as you work through your clearing out. They will help to keep your energy high.

Patting yourself on the back part way through

You can't always complete a task in one session but that doesn't mean your home has to be full of chaos relating to unfinished work. I first discovered the 'lint' instinct with my desk. People say that clutter breeds in the night and I don't think they are far wrong. For a long time, I didn't have a dedicated space in which to do my administration work. I had a drawer in which I kept my pens, stationery and some files, and I used to get them out and work on the dining table, so I was forced to clear them up when I was finished. Eventually, I realised I was avoiding doing my paperwork, because I couldn't be bothered to pull it all out, and rush to put it back before the next meal, so I invested in a proper desk and some drawer units and a filing cabinet. At first, because I didn't have to put things I was still working on away at the end of a work session, I left them out thinking that it was more efficient that way. I soon noticed that if I did that, the desk got more and more untidy, and cluttered with multiple items that were unconnected to the major project I was working on. I also noticed that eventually this untidiness spread to the whole room.

I went back to allowing only one project out on my desk at a time and always putting it away, even if incomplete, at the end of the day. Ironically, I discovered this made me feel more like picking it up again and completing it, even if it was something onerous like my end-of-year accounts, because I felt good about what I'd done so far and about my workspace in general. I found I unconsciously congratulated myself about getting that far as I put the project away for the night. Eventually, I developed systems that helped me remember tasks, deadlines, and incremental work on long-term projects, and that made me feel secure enough not to need visual reminders on my desk. We will cover these in the first home office chapter, if you need them. Many books on time management say that you should tidy your desk at the end of the day, and if mine is messy I will take a minute or two to do it, but I hardly ever have to. I am too addicted to the 'high' of patting myself on the back as I clear up after completing a particular stage in the project I'm working on. If there's no clearing up, there's no 'drawing a line' under it, and no congratulation.

Saying 'goodnight' to your house

I read an interview with respected journalist Joan Bakewell once, in which she was talking about how much she loved the house she'd lived in for decades. She lovingly described the following ritual, and I realised that I do it too. When I start to feel tired at the end of the evening and need to wind down quietly and give my mind the message that it is time to power down, I 'potter' about the house getting ready for bed. It only takes 10 minutes in all, but I go through the house putting things away in their proper places and pausing to feel the peace this produces in me whilst the kettle boils for my hot water bottle. There are usually no more than a few items out of place and, yes, I could leave it for the morning, and if I am really tired, I do. But if I do my ritual, my mind does power down because I know where everything goes and I don't really have to think. Then I go and take my make-up off and change for bed. I have heard this ritual compared to leaving the house 'ready for Santa' on Christmas eve. Whichever way you want to think of it, it is much nicer to wake up to order, rather than the sad remnants of a take-away or washing-up to do, and underlines the fact that the new day is a fresh start. On a more poetic level it is also a nice way of thanking the space for the way it has enabled you to do what you needed to all day. I find myself doing it in hotel rooms too.

The commercial break

If I have let things get messy in my house, which tends to happen if I've had to work when I'm too tired, then the following simple habit works wonders. I turn the television up and dash around in the commercial break putting away as much as I can before the programme starts again. If I'm not watching television I will set a timer, or play a favourite song to mark the time. It is amazing how much tidier you can make a room look in three minutes. It can feel so much better. Similarly, if I don't feel like starting on a project that I really need to do, I promise myself I will work on it for at least 10 minutes. I usually forget about the 10-minute deadline once I have started, and finish it without a thought.

Feel confident about letting things go

How do you know what to let go of and what to keep? Try asking yourself a few simple questions:

1   Do I need this item and use it regularly? And how
    often?
2   Do I absolutely love this item and does it enhance my
    life?
3   Do I have to store this item for legal/tax/business
    reasons, for the moment?

If you don't need it, or love it, or have to have it, then why
are you keeping it? You can clear an awful lot of stuff just
by walking around your house and asking yourself these
questions, without moving or reorganising anything. If
you have a lot of clutter, try going into one room and finding three items that you can part with immediately, and
then get rid of them, even if they are old pizza boxes full
of cold pizza... Feel better? Energetically, I think human
beings are a lot like snails. We know what we own and we
mentally carry all those possessions around with us, like
the snail with his shell. If there are too many, or some of
them are broken, mouldy, useless, ugly or make us sad, it
can make us feel weighed down. A special sub-category
here is items that you do need or use but which are in need
of repair. Put these aside to deal with, and please do it
promptly. Don't just put them back! They will jam up the
flow again if you do.

   I know this can feel scary, but when you are at this
point in the clutter-clearing process you will have to start
making decisions, and as quickly as possible. Set yourself
a time limit to go through a pile of papers or of other
possessions and stick to it. It is really tempting to start

reading old letters or worrying about what to do with whatever it is you have in your hand. Make a decision. I know the question for some of you will be 'What if I make the wrong decision?' You're a grown-up. You make lots of decisions all the time even if it is the decision that it is safe to ignore things and not make decisions, when in fact neglect can be far more damaging. You also have a 5 per cent error margin, remember? You are very unlikely to exceed this.

The other trap here is to decide that you will need an item without thinking about the specific occasion on which you will use it. Sometimes calling your own bluff on this will get you to see that it isn't worth keeping until then and that you would be better off throwing it away or recycling it. Sometimes, when you can't think of a specific occasion, it's because there isn't one. No backsliding now!

Follow through with decisions

When you are thinking about whether to keep an item, the next part of the process can flow on from that. If you decide you need it, you will also need to decide where it goes. If it belongs in another area or even another room, you will need to move it immediately. Additionally, you need to decide where you tend to use it and how often you need it. If it isn't fairly frequently you have two options. You can store it in the back of the nearest cupboard behind the most frequently used things. Or, if you don't have a good amount of storage space in that room, you would be better off storing it somewhere accessible until you next do, so that you can make space for items that it is essential to keep in that spot.

How and when to dispose of items you don't need

Once you have decided to get rid of an item, it is best to make an immediate decision about what to do with it. Are you going to:

1 Throw it away?
2 Recycle it?
3 Donate it to charity or friends?
4 Give it back to someone it belongs to, or who could use it?
5 Sell it?
6 Repair it?

I have listed the options in order of danger as you go down the list with the least risky at the top. If you are new to clearing clutter it is tempting to create new piles of stuff that you never get round to dealing with. *Make it a rule if you have had a clearing-out session that you put rubbish out immediately and put things to recycle or donate to charity or friends straight into the car.* The bigger your problem is, the more important it is that you do this. If your place is just overloaded with items on every surface and the floor, you are going to need lots of bin bags and to make as many trips to the dump or to the local charity shop as it takes. Congratulate yourself as you do this. If you need to return things, try to get that book, or whatever it is, back to whoever it belongs to as soon as you can. Put it in the post or whatever is quickest. And make a note in your diary or on your 'to do' list to take items for repair or renovation so that they can quickly be replaced where you will use them and get the benefit of them. If you end a clear-out with bags of stuff cluttering up your space for days afterwards, I'm afraid you didn't finish the job properly.

Creating order as you go

This may sound really obvious but, in my experience, it isn't. Start in one place, and clear systematically as you go. (There are exceptions to this rule and I will spell them out when necessary, but in general this principle works.) For instance, start in one corner of a room and pick each item up in sequence as you travel towards the next wall. Or if you are clearing using the principle of 'furthest away first', decide you are going to clear one shelf or one drawer or one cupboard and don't stop until you have. Once you pick an item up, you must deal with it and make a firm set of decisions about whether to keep it and what to do with it either way. Please don't defer a decision, and put it back down again. That is a very slippery slope. Remember to make the decision as quickly as you can and to keep the energy and your pace up. Also, however tempting it is, don't skip about the room tidying one thing here and another there (or even from room to room!) The reason for this is that if you stick to the place you are tidying and deal with things as you go, you will be creating order in your 'wake' and will be able to gain some visual satisfaction from this. You will also know where to pick up again after you are finished just for the moment, and when you want to come back to the task. If you skip about, you won't get the benefit of that visual satisfaction and that is disheartening. Moreover, what you will be doing, I'd guess, is picking off all the decisions that it's easy to make, and leaving the difficult ones or the ones you don't really want to face for later. Can you see what you would be doing there? You would be creating a 'wake' of difficult decisions that in the end will make it really hard for you to finish organising properly.

If you are the sort of person who has a fairly 'busy' tidiness style, don't panic! You can always add things later that make the space seem more 'cosy'. The point about doing it later is that it will be a conscious decision and you will have chosen things that you currently love. After all, tastes change. It is nice to change the feel of a room occasionally by changing the way it is dressed and giving yourself something new to look at. The main thing is, you won't have made a decision about what you live with, visually, by default.

So far, so good. What next?

Congratulations for getting this far. If you are looking to clear just one area of your house that is proving to be a problem, I recommend that you do the bathroom chapter as a warm-up and then read the relevant chapter for the area you want to clear. Many clutter books are written by people who are basically tidy, and they don't hold your hand enough through the clearing process. There are only a few principles here, but I am going to state them over and over each time you need to remember them, so that you don't forget and get stuck. Additionally, you will find all of them summarised in the two Appendices at the back of the book, for easy reference. You may find reading the rest of this chapter useful though, so that you fully understand the method I am using, as I will only be referring to my reasoning more briefly later on. You will also find the start of the chapter on storage spaces useful to go through if you need tips on learning to let go of things you don't need as it is here that you can first start to practise this skill. If you have a very small living space, for example, a studio flat, you will need to understand the principles in these first chapters very thoroughly and then apply them in conjunction with the special notes on small spaces in Chapter 10. If you experience problems once you have cleared a room, with recurring log jams, then try Chapter 13.

Where do you start?

So, if your entire home is a mess the big question is where to start. If you intend to clear the whole house or flat, the answer to this question is far from obvious. Most people's instinct is to create a transformation. This is very satisfying visually and may make you feel better about all the energy you had to expend, but it may actually be the source of your problem. If you wish to create great visual impact, then the obvious thing to do is to start with an area that you use every day, and to clear it. This seems like the most efficient thing to do, too. But what do you do with the items that you clear away? Chances are that if it has found its way to a heavy-traffic area, it isn't useless stuff. You probably do need it, but just not there and then. So what do you do with it? Shove it in a cupboard? Where? How do you know where to put it if it doesn't have a good place to live? If it did have a good place to live, I think that you would have put it there in the first place. Even if you do break the pattern here and relocate the item to the place where you will use it, you will probably find you have to stuff it into an already overfull cupboard, where it is hard to find and to access – and that just perpetuates the problem.

Many people trying to clear years of clutter find themselves in this bind, even if they don't have many of the myths and resistances of the previous chapters operating for them. They clear an area but they don't know where to put the things they clear. If they do, they find the space they'd like to put them in is full of useless stuff. So the item doesn't tend to get put back there every time and eventually finds its way back to the spot it was cluttering up in the first place. In the meantime our hero, or heroine, is tired and dispirited.

This is a hard pattern to break. And you have to take a bit of a fall in order to break it. You need to have a little patience and live with the chaos in your high-traffic area a little longer whilst you clear elsewhere. You have to clear from the least high-traffic areas first. You will be doing lots of hard work and not seeing the benefit for a while unless you persevere. That's so unfair, isn't it? But stay with me whilst I explain why I am asking you to do this the hard way.

Let's go back to the problem of what to do with the useful things you need to clear from a high-traffic area. Ideally, you need a well-organised storage space to store them in, close to the area where they will be needed. So how do you create these all over the house whilst you clear your high-traffic areas? Have you guessed? You clear the storage spaces first. If you decide to do this you will have to make a commitment to do a little and often with your clearing over the next few weeks. You won't be able to clear the whole house in one go. If you are the kind of person who needs to see a quick result in a couple of hours, then, with the exception of Chapter 2, this system is not for you. It has taken you years to create the clutter you have; you have placed it where it is piece by piece. You can't tidy it up if you expect it to stay that way, in a single afternoon. You are, in effect, creating new systems, blueprints and habits around the way you store and access your things, and that takes time.

That's the bad news. The good news is that if you are willing to schedule in regular clearing sessions and to establish a few new habits, then it can most definitely be done in the space of a few weeks.

So, with the exception of the warm-up chapter on bathrooms, through which you can get sense of how the whole system works, we are going to start with the storage spaces furthest away from your everyday living space first: your attics, garages and junk rooms. And no, even though it will probably take you quite a while to clear and order these spaces, you won't see the benefit within your living space immediately. Sorry. Attics, garages and junk rooms are actually relatively easy spaces for you to learn your first good habits in, and these will stand you in good stead when you come to clear your living spaces. They're a good way to warm up for the main event. After all, the point is not so much the clearing out, but learning how to live clutter- free.

Chapter seven
Storage spaces

If you want your clutter clearing to last, storage spaces are the best place to start. This is because you want to have clear, well-organised spaces for things that you need to keep, near to where you will use them. They are also a good place to start from the point of view of retraining yourself, because the main thing you need to do in them is let go of things, and this is also the first thing you need to learn. Zoning is not as important in these spaces as it is in a 'heavy-traffic' area of your house, such as the kitchen, which has to be really well organised to stay tidy and yet be in use all day, every day. Completion is also less important (other than initially completing the section you intended to clear) because you won't be visiting this space very often. As we move on to the more well-used areas of your house, we will be applying all three ideas at once. For the moment then, use the time you take to clear your storage spaces to become good at letting go of the things you don't really need.

Pick a space

Firstly, pick a space to clear and allow sufficient time to do this. If you are intending to clear your whole home, you should ideally pick the one that is most neglected, least used and furthest away from your heavy-traffic living areas. If you think you will need a day, then schedule your clear-out for the weekend, so that if the task spills over into the next day you are not living with the mess for a week until you can tackle it again. If you don't have a lot of time, clear a corner, a certain pile or even a crate or drawer.

Learning to let go

You are going to do one of five things with the items you find in your storage space:

- Keep them.
- Throw them away.
- Donate them to charity.
- Recycle them.
- Relocate them.

Be aware that some of the things you find here may have very strong emotions attached to them, and that you will probably find this exercise more tiring than you thought it would be. There will also probably be a high volume of items that you are going to throw out or donate, so you need to be prepared to move these items as fast as possible out of your space, and to make plans for doing so as part of the clearing process. In other words, until you have done this, you haven't finished clearing.

Make a start

This is the first of many times I will say this. Having decided on the area you are clearing (even if it is only one corner of your attic or one crate in your garage) pick up the first item, and make a decision. These are the four questions that I will repeat throughout the book to help you make this decision:

- Do I really need this item and regularly use it? And when?
- Where do I tend to use this item and how often?
- Do I absolutely love this item and does it enhance my life?
- Do I need to keep this item for legal reasons or because of some other obligation?

Let's look at these questions in some more depth.

■ Do I really need this item and regularly use it? And when?

No cheating here. If you haven't used this item in the last two years and its use isn't confined to a specialist occasion or purpose that's likely to come up, then you probably don't need it. If you have a surfboard and haven't used it but someone has invited you to Hawaii for surfing (or you are diligently saving so that you can go) then you are quite right to keep it for that occasion. But if not, if you were planning to take the train to Cornwall to surf but you never have, are you harbouring fantasies about how elastic time is for you? Do you imagine that 'someday' you will have time to use it? You probably won't. You have already spent the last two years prioritising other things over using this item. Be honest with yourself, let it go and move on. You really will feel better afterwards.

Something that it's also crucial to consider here is *when* you will next need this item. If you have a small office and only use certain pieces of equipment infrequently, is it really worth having them on top of you all the time? It may be better putting them somewhere else until they're needed. Similarly, with summer clothes: if your bedroom is tiny but you have an attic, store them there. And if the answer to 'When?' is 'Oh sometime...' you will just be kidding yourself and you won't know where to store the item either, because the place where it should be stored is based on a prediction of when you will use it. Get rid of it!

■ Where do I tend to use this item and how often?
Where you use an item, and how often, will determine where it should be stored. This question becomes more crucial when you are clearing living spaces, but it's as well to consider it here too. I will cover this in more detail in the chapters that deal with any specific living space. For the moment, though, it will get you thinking about whether anything in a storage space needs to be

moved elsewhere, where you can use it more easily and more often.

■ Do I absolutely love this item and does it enhance my life?

The trap with this question is thinking that every item kept for sentimental reasons is life enhancing or associated with a positive emotion. Many things that evoke powerful feelings are often kept because the owner hasn't been able to let go or to face the sadness that they will experience if they look at the item properly. There is no short cut here. If you aren't ready to let go then you don't have to. But try to limit the number of items with which you do this. If it makes you feel unhappy, do you really want to leave that little 'bomb' of sadness around to catch you out unawares every time you come across it? Be brave. Hold a little ceremony to burn the item if necessary (safely of course) but try to deal with it properly. The likelihood is that you can let it go if you really try. And if an item you've kept for sentimental reasons makes you feel good, what is it doing in a dusty storage space and not out where you can enjoy it? If you can display it, then it can do its job of reminding you of good times or of something of which you are proud.

I know people who say that they keep their connection to loved ones by retaining what those loved ones have given them. Don't let this be a substitute for really staying in touch with loved family or friends and spending meaningful time with them. Some people find it helpful to take photos of a sentimental object so that they still have it in some form and then they can let the object go.

■ Do I need to keep this item for legal reasons or because of some other obligation?

Beware of storing things for other people for indefinite periods. Remember this is your space. If you have to, and there is a lot of material, consider storing it somewhere else at a storage facility. If you need to keep things for legal reasons then make sure you really need to retain them. Accounts can be shredded after seven years, and there is often surprisingly little that you need to hang on to in your archives. Store all the items in each category together, i.e. tax and accounts, contracts, etc., or all your daughter's furniture. You should be very clear about how much space these items take up and where they are. You can only do that if it is all neatly stored together out of the way. Where should you store them? Somewhere that is very much off the beaten path of your living space. So if you have a little mezzanine attic in your office space but are likely to need to store lots of paperwork and promotional materials where you can reach them easily, then that isn't a good place to store your daughter's furniture: this space is too precious to you. But if your office is a large space and you have plenty of storage closer to your desk, then it is.

Keep going and follow through

Pick up the next item and make a decision using the four questions detailed above. And then the next, and the next, until you have cleared out all of that area. You are creating a 'wake' of order. It is fatal to pick something up and defer making a decision. That will just cause terrible confusion. Keep asking yourself the questions and remember that you are allowed a few mistakes. The chances are, though, that you didn't know half this stuff was stored here, and that if you put it back you'll live happily without it for a good while or even forever! If you think you can utilise an item now, promote it by moving it into the room in the house where it will be made fit for use (i.e. cleaned or mended) or into the room where it will be used. If you wish to continue storing it, put it on one side. Throw anything you don't need into the rubbish bag or the 'to donate' charity bag or the 'recycle' bag and put these three bags into your car at the end of the process to dispose of as soon as possible.

What to do with what's left

With items you decide to keep, label them well and store them in protective materials and try to put like with like. This is the one time I will tell you to do that. It is because these aren't living spaces and they don't have to support any tasks that you do. They are purely for storage and are not going to be accessed that often, so arranging by function doesn't make sense here because it isn't needed.

Are you a bit loath to fill storage spaces properly? Are you one of those people with empty attics who can't find your telephone or your kitchen table? Think about why you have this instinct. We know that you are not going to 'lose' your stuff if you put it away. An awful lot of the stuff you currently have cluttering up your living space is not useful or precious enough to actually justify it being stored there. Banish it to somewhere less precious!

Well done! Did you clear a drawer or a crate and not overwhelm and tire yourself? Well done for that. Did you find that you wanted to go on a bit longer and clear one more drawer whilst you were in the flow? Good. That is a great instinct to cultivate. Ideally, you should finish a clutter-clearing session by glancing at how far along the pile or wall you have got, and appreciating the sight of all that 'order', and feel that you really would like to come back to it soon to complete it.

Put anything you decided to continue storing away neatly and where it can be accessed if it needs to be. There really shouldn't be too much of this stuff now. You should be left with quite a lot of space for storing other things that you need occasionally but which are currently cluttering up your living space. Keep scheduling small sessions, if necessary, until the whole attic or outbuilding is cleared.

Keep going through the house

Now you need to focus on all the other storage areas in your house in order of the least used first: consider the understairs cupboard, the attic (if not cleared already), the potting shed, the cellar, the garage, the junk room. All these areas will fall into one of two categories:

- Spaces that you would like to use purely for storage.
- Spaces that are primarily for storage but where you also fulfil a task.

Clear the storage-only areas first and only put back what you really need to keep in there because you don't use it very often, such as Christmas decorations, for example, or all your decorating gear. Storage areas that also fulfil a function would include potting sheds, where you also do some basic gardening tasks such as sowing seeds. I recommend you clear living spaces first, before you tackle these. You can go back to them later and by then you will have understood the principles enough to whizz through them. Remember to 'promote' items that would be better to store in an active work zone, to near where the task gets done, so that you can get to them later.

Chapter eight
Bedrooms

Your bedroom has a few basic functions: you sleep there, dress there, groom yourself there, perhaps you watch television, read or work in bed on your laptop. It should ideally be a harmonious and uncluttered space where you can wind down and sleep well at the end of the day. As with all the rooms in your house, it also has to be geared to the way you use the space as an individual. So if you need to study in your bedroom you will put your books in a very different place to where you may put them if all you do is read to help you fall asleep.

Plan first

As we move back into sorting out the rooms you use every day, the principles of zoning and completion come back into play. We have to do this to make sure that the system has the best chance of staying in place once it is set up. As any good carpenter will tell you, 'Measure twice, cut once...' We need to make sure that you have got your thinking right on the zoning and completion concepts, so, as in the bathroom chapter, we are going to start with a plan.

Firstly, think about the natural zones in your room. Walk into your bedroom and consider the tasks you do in there and where you do them. Where do you dress? Where do you actually stand when you do this? Where do you brush your hair or do your make-up? Is this the best place in terms of light? Is your bed positioned well? Or have you always had a yearning to have it closer to the window so that you can look out when you wake up in the morning? Where do you read? Study? Watch TV? Did you form a mental picture of this space from the visualising exercise? How you would like this room to look? Call that image up again and bear it in mind now.

For each of your tasks, think about what you need to hand to accomplish them and whether those items are all together. You are aiming to create efficient 'zones': one for general grooming, one for dressing, one for study and so forth. For the moment, decide where these zones will be for you and whoever else uses the room, listing them on paper if necessary.

Starting to organise the space

Now start in one corner of the room and work in a systematic way, sorting out items as you go. Pick each item up and make a decision. Remember to ask yourself the basic questions:

1   Do I need this item and use it regularly? And when?

2   Where do I tend to use it and how often?
3   Do I absolutely love this item and does it enhance
    my life?
4   Do I absolutely have to store this item for the moment?

Now with each item, throw it away, decide to give it away,
or if you keep it, put it in its proper 'zone' or even in
another room if it belongs there. If the place to which you
are relocating the item is not organised yet, don't worry,
because you are going to tackle that later. If it *is* organised
then put the item in its correct place. Don't be tempted to
switch rooms.

   If you are storing a set of things do they have to take up
valuable living space here? Could they be kept somewhere
out of the way in another less lived-in part of the house?
Keep working your way systematically as you go. When
you get to the end of one wall, go back and put things away
so that it is easy to access them when you are using that
zone. Put items that you commonly use every day at the
front of shelves, etc. The idea, as always, is to create a zone
where you dress for instance: where you can just reach out
and find underwear, thermals (I get cold, okay?), suitable
clothes and shoes all in one go. If you have a strapless bra
that you only wear with your ballgown then obviously this
will go to the bottom or the back of the underwear drawer
but if you go to a regular dance class then your sports bra
will live somewhere near the front. Don't try to use the
space 'efficiently' by cramming everything into one drawer.
Make things easy to locate, access and put away, leaving

extra space to differentiate between them if necessary. And don't panic if you have some space left.

If your storage areas in the bedroom are completely overflowing so that you can't put things away properly, then you will have to target them individually first and before you start trying to create a wake of order. You will need to aim to purge as much as you can (not forgetting to get these items out of the house as soon as possible). Then, when you've created some space in your cupboards and other storage areas, you can start replacing items in their correct zones but out of sight. If the number of clothes you have is a problem, see the next part of this chapter where I have outlined how to prune your wardrobe and make it twice as effective.

Think very carefully about the pictures and ornaments that you keep. This room is supposed to be restful. Try to limit the number of these unless you can't live without 'stuff' making the place seem 'cosy'. Remember it will look tidier and more harmonious if the ornaments are all in the same style or in the same colours, but of course whether you choose to limit yourself like this will depend on your personal taste. I will say again here that visual clutter is fine if you love it and it makes you feel good, and it isn't hampering you in the way that you use the room.

Ease of use

Next, consider where you should put things for ease of use. So if you watch television in bed, for example, make sure that you can see the screen easily from where you lie and try keeping the remote on the bedside table, because that's where you'll use it. Think about what's missing. Do you have enough storage to be able to put what you want to keep away easily? And are you missing an item? For instance, a good mirror near the window where you do your hair? If you only have one on the other side of the room you'll find your hairbrushes and other items 'migrating' back because that's where you tend to use them. Get a new mirror or move the old one, or relocate the zone...

Once you have finished sorting out this room, aim to put things away in their proper places (now that they have one...) as you go. You will need that completion habit to make things stay clear in here. If you don't manage this, spend a few minutes putting things away when you are dressed and making your bed in the morning.

Your wardrobe

This storage item is approached separately because it is so large a project and will take you quite a while to complete. There is a simple organising principle here. It is that everything in your wardrobe should be loved, fit to wear and easy to find.

■ Fit to wear

If your heart sinks when you open your wardrobe door it may be because you are actually offering yourself a lot of non-starters or fake choices mixed in with the real ones. This makes seeing good combinations of clothes much harder. When you look in your wardrobe, your mind has to make a quick assessment of what is in there and decide which garments are not really usable right now. It does this and discards these items as true options, often below your consciousness. Your mind is often busy and taken up with doing this, whilst you think what you are doing is offering it a lot of real choices. That's really confusing!

■ Easy to find

How do you know how many white shirts you have? Or skirts, tops, pairs of black shoes or black trousers? If I asked you to answer those questions you would probably group all these items together. This is so that you can see at a glance how many you have almost without even having to count. Moreover, if there is a significant item that is missing, your eye will spot it pretty quickly. We are going to use this tendency to your advantage as we reorganise your wardrobe to make it easier for you to use.

■ Branding exercise

As usual we are going to gain a little clarity on your own personal objective first. This is a much-condensed version of an exercise I discovered in a marvellous book called *10 Steps to Fashion Freedom*. If you are serious about dressing well then I highly recommend that you get it and do all the exercises in it.

First of all, have a think about how things are sold to you every day. Aren't there words that you associate with certain products and that you have done for decades? For example, Ford – isn't the word there 'reliability'? But with

Ferrari, isn't it 'flair'? And with Armani, isn't it 'elegance'? Advertisers have put a lot of money and many hours of work into making sure that these products have these connotations and that they stay in your mind.

What you may not have realised is that this works with people too. What does the Queen bring to mind – wealth, power and continuity? What about Stephen Fry – do you think of witty and erudite? And Audrey Hepburn – do the words elegance and grace come to mind? The way each of these people dresses (or dressed) underlines these qualities. Your wardrobe is already giving out a message about how you think of yourself and may be teaching others how to regard you. Yes, I know this tendency is facile, but do you think the average human psyche has the strength to resist the hundreds of messages it is given via advertising every day that looks matter, in the split second it has to weigh you up? I am not talking about becoming a raving beauty or a 'fashion icon' here, I am talking about what your clothes say about your expectations in life and your opinion of yourself. There is no such thing as a non statement in this regard. If you don't agree that clothes matter, then your statement is one of rebellion and that in itself may make others uneasy.

It is essential that you decide on an image that you feel fits you well. Doing so provides a filter for the decisions you make about what to keep and, later on, what to buy. Without it, it is very easy to get lost, and if you have a huge wardrobe, it can make sorting it out nigh on impossible, especially if you *are* a beauty and look good in pretty much everything. If you find yourself resisting this process, take a little time first to find out where your resistance lies and ask yourself if you can deal with your issue in some other way. Then:

1   Find some words that you think would describe you best. Have fun with this and be complimentary... Are you unconventional? Do you have flair? Are you elegant? Reliable? Glamorous? Friendly and warm-hearted? Wacky? Charismatic? Have you always wished to be regarded differently? Do you want to change your image? Now's your chance. Each of the words you choose will have other connotations. 'Elegant' can encompass 'Noble' or 'Refined' or 'Authoritative'. Write a list of meanings for each of your chosen words.

2   Whittle your list down to three essential words. Place them in the sentence: My image is that of someone _____, _____ and _____. This is your 'slogan' and is the essence of your 'brand'.

3   Memorise your phrase. You will need it every day from now on. If you can't decide conclusively, settle on your best choice. You can always amend it later.

■ Wardrobe clearing

Start your clearing out by setting aside an afternoon (or longer if necessary) to try on and go through every item in your wardrobe. Ask an honest and kindly friend to help you if you need to. Begin at one end of the rail. Pick the item up, try it on and ask the following questions about it.

1 Does it fit?
2 Does it suit my colouring and my current style? (You
   know what this is now because all you have to do is
   repeat your slogan ... does this item fit in with it or
   not? A feather boa is not going to make you look reliable! But there are much subtler things to look out for
   such as quality and cut and colour that even in the
   average article, will convey other messages.)
3 Does it make me feel good?
4 Does it need altering, repairing or dyeing (or cleaning!) to make it completely right?

Enlist your friend to help you answer these questions and
only if the item gets a 'yes' for the first three questions can
it go back on the rail at the same end. If it gets a yes to
question 4 then put it aside in one of two (or three) piles.
These are:

1 Alterations or repairs you will make yourself.
2 Alterations or repairs you will have made by someone
   else.
3 Items to have cleaned.

If you are handy with a needle and really do put time aside
to make clothes then by all means put an item that you
will remake on the 'alteration' pile. Go through each item
in turn making decisions as you go. Don't skip items to
come back to later (when you're tired!) and do replace
each garment at the same end of the rail so that you know

what you have tried on and what you haven't. Discard anything that doesn't pass the test. You can sell these clothes or give them to charity or to your friends. If you are having trouble letting them go, then read Chapter 5: Myths and bad habits again. I recommend that you take the fastest route to getting the clothes you decide to discard out of your home. It would be fatal to let them clutter up some other corner because you haven't got round to disposing of them yet. You are new to this process so cut yourself a bit of slack and take the easy option. Put the clothes straight in your car to drop off next time you are at the charity shop if you can. Eventually, you will get to the end of the rail. Do the same process now with shoes and with all the clothing stored in drawers. Remember to leave lots of time for this ... possibly another whole clearing session.

If you find yourself getting stuck on a particular piece, here are some additional questions to ask yourself:

- Will I really wear this item? When? Where? How often? How many other items in my wardrobe does it go with? Does it make me look good? Is it one of those garments that looks really good on me but is now looking very worn? (If this is so, and it can't be mended, let it go. You don't want to look scruffy.)
- Is what this garment transmits about its wearer really what I want to tell the world about myself, right now? Things change. Bright waistcoats or cute flowers may have suited you a decade ago but do they say who you

are and who you want to be now? Maybe you are in your thirties and want to be taken seriously now. Maybe you are in your sixties and you don't! Does it make *you* look good? (Not Angelina Jolie, or Johnny Depp, or your best friend who is a completely different size and shape... But you as you currently are?)

• Is there a particular occasion that I need this garment for? Do you travel in the tropics? Attend formal dinners? Business meetings? Go hill walking? If it is very specialist and expensive and you will need it for one of these occasions I recommend that you keep it, but hopefully it will scream your slogan as well. If it doesn't, when that item needs replacing, get a garment that does.

If you find yourself getting completely stuck on this exercise, try putting the garments you wear the most often on one side of the rail. Chances are it is the same five or six items. This is the *actual* size of your useful wardrobe, so ask yourself: why are you keeping the rest? If you can, pick out some other pieces and ask yourself why you aren't using them and what you could do to make them more useful. It is much better to know what you have and what you actually use, than to preserve the illusion that you have a lot of good clothes, and still feel that you have nothing to wear in the morning.

■ What to do with what's left
Sort the things that are left on the rail in order of colour and type. So at one end, all the black suits followed by all

the black shirts/tops, then all the grey trousers and all the grey shirts/tops, and so forth. You may want to put categories of clothes together, for instance, specialist clothes for work, or all your summer dresses, but I recommend using the colour system.

Having done the exercise, look at the rail. Two things will be apparent. One is that you know that *every item on this rail makes you look and feel good and is ready to go*. In other words, what you are looking at is a real choice. The other thing is that it will suddenly be obvious that you have bought 15 pairs of jeans but have no tops to wear with them, or that you have some smart suits for work, but no shoes that match. The gaps in your wardrobe will show.

One reason why you might have felt that you have nothing to wear is these gaps. Have a look at what is missing. Sometimes, if you just buy one jacket or one pair of trousers to help unify the elements you already have, you find that you have a lot more combinations available to you. My guess is that if you've been opening a wardrobe full of unsorted clothes and feeling that you had nothing to wear, that at the end of this process you will find that actually, you were right. In other words, that the number of complete combinations of well-fitting good-quality clothes in your wardrobe was not enough and were hard to see, amongst all the other stuff in there that wasn't working for you.

Take a little time, now, to pick out new combinations of clothes that scream your slogan and that might work for a specific occasion. What would you wear to a business lunch for instance, or your Pilates class, or to go Breton dancing? Sometimes, finding a new way to wear an old favourite is as satisfying as buying a new item. Now that you can locate items more easily, this should be much easier to do and can, paradoxically, make you feel that you have more items in your wardrobe than before you threw anything out!

To finish off this exercise, take the items to be dyed or altered or cleaned to the appropriate places, get them dealt with and replace them in your wardrobe as soon as you can. If you find yourself with only three outfits or suits that fit properly, look good on you and are decent to wear, then you will have to do some shopping. Make a list of the types of occasions you need more clothes for, whether it's for the office or going out to the opera, and then make a list of what you will need. Try to use your slogan as you shop unless what you have to wear is very proscribed indeed and you have no choice at all. What you may find is, now that you know your slogan and how useful an item is likely to be, that you can confidently spend more on it. It is better to invest in one well-cut garment that screams 'quality' and fits in well with two or three of your key colours or looks, than half a dozen that scream 'cheap'. Don't forget to store each item by colour, etc., and to have any initial alterations necessary done as quickly as is practical (sometimes clothes shops do alterations or a good local dry cleaners often has this facility) so that you can enjoy what you have bought as soon as possible.

If you really take the time to follow through with trying out new combinations and shopping with your slogan in mind, you will find that you become increasingly confident about what you wear on any occasion. It will be much harder for you to be caught out.

Travel and packing

I'm going to include a short section on this, whilst we're discussing shopping and wardrobes. It is a really good idea to base your wardrobe around two or three neutral colours that can each form the basis of a 'capsule' wardrobe when you go away. It makes packing far easier. In fact, the weeding out that you have been doing, and placing garments of the same colour together, should have encouraged you to see your wardrobe in terms of these neutrals as a basic foundation, and what goes with them. You will probably already have found that you have a lot of black (or brown) pieces.

For instance, like many women, I have lots of well-cut basic items in black, such as trousers, skirts and tops that can be livened up with a few showier and more colourful items. My black 'capsule' clothes are also cold-weather ones as I hate wearing black when the sun comes out. This makes it easier to make sure that I have shoes and coats and cardigans to match most of the items in this range. My black clothes include items suitable for business meetings or going to parties. My cream 'capsule' is designed to look more summery but cope with our treacherously chilly and sometimes wet summer weather in the UK. It includes items such as long linen skirts and trousers under which I can still hide cream-coloured silk thermals, and a linen and wool cream coat that I can throw over myself as soon as the sun goes down and the temperature starts to drop. Footwear includes a choice of warm suede boots, or sandals, so that I am covered if I pack these two items. As a professional singer, this capsule is what I reach for when I am going to a festival to perform as it mixes and matches with my stage outfits very easily. My white 'capsule' clothes are tropical and of the thinnest cotton with some lovely prints. They match all my swimsuits and holiday gear.

Shopping for items that will expand the range of a set of existing neutrals that you have, can really open up the number of combinations in your wardrobe and help you to cut down on packing. If you base each of these around a specific type of weather you can be even more efficient. I don't buy black sandals, for instance, as I know I won't ever use them. Similarly, I know I am unlikely ever to need white boots. As soon as I am going away, all I have to think about is what the temperature is likely to be where I am going, to have a fairly instant idea of what I will pack, and be confident that it will all work together. Knowing your wardrobe this well also means that you don't have to reach for 'safe and boring' when buying travel clothes. You can choose brightly coloured or stylish items knowing how they will fit in with the rest of your neutrals and how many combinations you can get out of them.

Try to buy items that will wash and dry easily where you can, and that will be forgiving with creases. It's not easy to acquire a really adaptable capsule wardrobe instantly. You're far more likely to be able to create one if you bear these principles in mind every time you add to your wardrobe. Oh, and if you are one of those people who are addicted to travel-size toiletries, store them in a bag in your suitcase so that you don't forget to use them when you go away.

Maintenance

You will have guessed by now what I am going to ask, won't you? Make it a rule never to put anything dirty, shabby or unmended back into your wardrobe. When you do put an item back, use the extra three seconds it will take you to put it back in the section in which it belongs, by colour and category. That way your wardrobe will stay organised without any effort. When you go shopping, think about items that will give you more opportunities to wear what you already have in a new way. A good purchase will go with several items that you already have and be part of several 'looks'. Remember to repeat your slogan whenever you're in the shop trying things on. It is a great way to keep yourself grounded in a sale or when you're in a hurry. If the item isn't the epitome of the words in your slogan, step away from the till...

Keep maintaining the rest of your bedroom, too, simply by putting things back where they belong first time. If you buy a new item remember to make a decision about where and how frequently you will use it so that you can place it correctly in its zone. New wardrobe items should immediately be placed in the correct section. This is so simple and yet so important. If you neglect it, however, all is not lost. The fact that everything has a good place to be will help you put it back easily. Play your favourite song and see if you can get the room cleared by the time it has finished. Bedrooms are about nurturing and rest. If you are finding it easier to feel well rested in yours when it is tidy, then that is the obvious incentive to keep it that way.

Handbags

Women's clothing is often designed without useful pockets. Dress trousers or trousers bought with a suit will often not include pockets and sometimes jackets don't either. Women can get bogged down with that 'just in case' instinct to carry more and more things in their bags (especially if you are a Mum) until carrying it distorts their whole body. What is worse is the way that if you need something from the bottom of the bag, you have to tip the entire contents out to find it. Bags that have a wider base than the top are useful 'bottomless pits' in this respect. They carry huge amounts of items, which is great, but finding anything in them can be murder. It is easy to start 'living' out of your bag, almost. Never wanting to check if there is anything you could leave behind because it would take so long and you are afraid of forgetting something. And never clearing it out, let alone cleaning it.

If, like me, you are someone who likes to be prepared for anything, an easier way to deal with this is to use smaller bags to sort things by category (i.e. function) and then to place them in your handbag. I tend to use pencil cases, or A6 size make-up bags in clear mesh if I can get them, as they are hard-wearing and easy to check visually. One of these houses all the homeopathic remedies I like to carry around for instance, another is a touch-up bag for make-up. You could have one for a very small stationery kit if you use your car as an office sometimes, or one for all those 'just in case things' such as ear plugs, paracetamol, medication you regularly take and your contact lens case. You could also have a larger one with wipes and a spare toy and nappies, etc., if you are going out with your child, which remains perpetually replenished and packed so that you can be more spontaneous with them. It makes changing handbags much simpler and easier as you only have to move your 'sub-bags' without worrying too much that you're going to miss some small item. If there is a whole category of things you won't need that day, such as your stationery for instance, it is easy to omit that sub-bag. It also makes everything easier to find. Do you think Audrey Hepburn or Princess Grace of Monaco (or whoever your epitome of elegance and style is) ever had to go rooting around noisily in their handbag to find something, or even worse, tip the entire contents out on to the table? Of course not! Unthinkable!

(Just kidding... They never do in your fantasies about them, though, do they?)

Make-up

Make-up has 'use by' dates. If you are at all unsure, you should throw out any items that are old, and especially those that you use near your eyes, such as mascara. If you are one of those people who compulsively buys and hoards make-up, consider doing a separate 'branding' exercise with regard to your look. You will need to repeat this every few years. All of us need to reassess our make-up as we get older, not just because our faces get more wrinkly but because, even in our twenties and thirties, our colouring and the image we want to project changes.

What do you want your make-up to do for you and to convey? If you want to be attractive to prospective partners remember that natural beauty (strategically and subtly enhanced of course!) is what attracts most people of all ages, genders and orientations. Thick make-up can make a face look too covered and 'sticky' to be caressed or kissed. And that is, after all, what you really want, isn't it? It is likely to make you look very 'hard-edged' and intimidating too. I know some women want to use that effect as a defence. It can feel as though heavy make-up acts as a protection, or stops people noticing your physical flaws (and I speak as an ex-addict here, who would fully make-up for a 6am transfer to the airport...) but in fact it doesn't. Start by asking those around you, whose judgement you trust, what they think about your look. Try going without make-up (or reducing it) and gauging the reaction of others to you. Most importantly, *listen*. Make a decision about that for yourself now, so that you can weed out the products that you don't need, on your dressing table.

Try to limit the number of 'special-occasion' and 'just-in-case' products. And if you find yourself slavishly buying expensive perfumes or products because of some celebrity connotation or endorsement, ask yourself if you actually use all those products regularly and whether they make *you* look good. Do they enhance your own beauty? If they don't, you know what I am going to say. Forgive yourself and throw them out. If they don't enhance you and you still compulsively buy them, try going back to read the section in Chapter 5 on 'buying hope'. I think you are possibly wasting your hard-earned cash on 'stardust' that you think will rub off. Sadly, it won't. The only way to attract people or to be charismatic or special is to make those elusive qualities for yourself. I switched from Estée Lauder, Lancôme, Mac and Chanel, wherever I could find the right colours, to Tesco's own brand for the majority of my make-up a couple of years ago... And no one has noticed!

Chapter nine
Kitchens

I'm guessing that you have some semblance of order in here even if you exist on takeaways, otherwise you wouldn't have any plates to eat them off. What you can do is extend this system and make your kitchen much easier to clean and to keep tidy.

Tasks in the kitchen

First, as usual, establish your zones by thinking about the way you function in your kitchen. The everyday tasks you have to be free to do unhampered are fairly obvious and standard.

- Cooking
- Washing-up
- Making drinks

You may also use your kitchen to:

- Eat (if there's a table)
- Socialise

- Do homework
- Do laundry
- Open the post

In addition you may use it to store the recycling as well as food and crockery and pans and other goods.

Think about where on the counter you tend to prepare raw food. Also look at which section of the counter you normally serve it. Remember where you dump the washing-up before you are ready to tackle it. And where you put the kettle and make the tea or coffee. Consider where the washing machine and the dryer are housed (if they are in the kitchen). How close is the dishwasher to where you either clear plates or store crockery? Each of these places is a mini workstation for a task that is frequently repeated. All the items you need to accomplish each task should be near the appropriate space or they will tend not to get put back, except if you are opening your house for a cover story in *House and Garden*, or if your in-laws are coming to stay... (I don't know which would be more stressful!) This means that with this room you will have to be especially good at 'promoting' and 'demoting' items once you ask yourself where and how often you use them. Items are used so frequently here that if you don't do this accurately you will build up log jams very quickly in the ensuing weeks.

Getting started

Let's get back to the basic functions and tasks in your kitchen. Where do you prepare foods for cooking and assemble ingredients? Start clearing out by picking a cupboard furthest away from this part of the kitchen. This is because as usual you are going to create storage space as you clear and I want you to have a place in which to put all those obscure jelly moulds and piping bags that you decide to keep but will only use occasionally. Pick the highest or the most neglected cupboard.

Take each item out as you put your hand on it and ask yourself five questions each time:

1   Do I need this item and use it regularly? And when?
2   Where do I tend to use it and how often?
3   Do I absolutely love it?
4   Is it in good repair?
5   Do I need to keep it but move it elsewhere?

Kitchens tend to collect dreams and aspirations about our domestic selves. They are often stuffed with things that would be essential if we ever got round to doing that domestic god/dess thing. Old jars for making your own chutney, food processors that gather dust, gadgets for frothing hot chocolate (I've still got mine and I really should get rid of it because I never use it) ... the list is endless. As you clear out, try to be realistic about what you have actually used in, say, the last two years and try to be kind to yourself. If you refuse to let go of any of your cooking gadgets then you are actually putting a pressure on yourself to find time to use them fairly regularly, and you will carry that thought subconsciously. This can fuel a low-grade feeling that you never actually achieve enough, when what is really happening is that you may have decided (very sensibly) to prioritise other important stuff such as listening to your partner or building your business rather than baking your own biscuits. If this has to be the priority in your life then remember to let yourself off the hook! I am not trying to downgrade the idea of keeping equipment if you love to cook. If you are a great cook then you are very justified in keeping whatever you regularly use. There is a trend, though, for many of us to watch 'gastro porn', and because feeding ourselves and others is such a fundamental activity, we can be less than honest with ourselves about how much we actually do cook.

Similarly, with endless tea sets or dinner services or pans, think about how much crockery you use regularly and keep this plus anything special that you don't wish to sell. Give the rest away and let someone else enjoy it. The kitchen is also a place in which duplicates of things hide, hoping never to be rumbled... Unless you regularly cook with your kids or your partner or friends, you don't need that many kitchen knives and whisks unless they are of different sizes and genuinely fulfil different functions. If you do, only keep the extras, which, realistically, you will need.

Pick each item up and decide whether to throw it away, or give it away or sell it. If it doesn't fit with a task you do in the kitchen then put it in the room in which it will be used. As you finish clearing a cupboard put back the items that are seldom used first, but don't stuff them so full that you have to lift lots of items out of the way to get to things at the back. Put the more frequently used items at the front and try even at this stage to relocate things to where they are most likely to be used. So if you discover a lovely teapot that you didn't know you had and decide you are going to use it regularly, don't put it back in the overhead cupboard by the door where you discovered it. Put it by the tea caddy for now and find a place for it when you clear the cupboards by them, when you get to that point. Keep doing this as you clear and as you go. This is why it is important to have thought about where your various zones are, first.

■ Keep going

Keep on clearing out each obscure cupboard or storage area, in order of the most obscure first. Tackle one area at a time so that you can finish it before moving on, and remember to make a decision on each thing you pick up before you move on to the next one. Eventually, you will get to the more precious storage areas around your cooker and sink and fridge. As you clear these remember to demote items that you don't use in this part of the kitchen or don't use very often to those now more spacious obscure cupboards. Think of it like a very strict system of postcodes. Stockwell may only be a couple of miles from Mayfair, but that makes all the difference to the price of a one-bedroom flat! Remember that the cupboards close to where you serve and prepare food really have to work for their existence. When you put items back in them, make sure that every one is still easy to reach and access. The kitchen is a place where, as you get to this premium space, it is particularly important not to fill your cupboards with as much stuff as you can stack in them. That just won't work in the long term. Things need to be easy to reach and access because they are so frequently used.

Try to keep grouping items according to where they will be used. Pans should be close to the stove unless they are specialist ones and you don't use them that often. Crockery that you tend to use every day should be close to the area where you serve your food, or the dishwasher, and your special sets can be stored either in the dining room or further away from this surface. And you have thrown out or given away that juicer you never use by now, haven't you?

■ Other items

Recycling can really take over. Invest in some large plastic crates or even bins to put tins, paper, glass and compost, etc., in, if your local council doesn't provide these, or what they provide is not enough. Try to make a good space for them where you won't trip over them and where they are not getting in the way of your more important kitchen tasks. Consider moving them to a porch or somewhere less in the way, but where you can still access them easily. Make them easy to use and large enough that they look tidy most of the time. Empty them often and in between collection, if necessary, to keep them that way.

Cleaning materials should all live under the sink and the washing powder and conditioner near the washing machine if it is sited much further away. If you have too many for one shelf, store products that double up on the same job away somewhere and use them up as you go. (You aren't starting a chemicals factory, are you!)

■ Work surfaces

Finally, we come to the work surfaces. By now, hopefully you will have created space, even in those premium cupboards, in which you can store things. Have a look at what is out on the surfaces in your kitchen. If there are things here relating to tasks that are done elsewhere in the house, move them now. Yes, this means moving that huge pile of papers by the telephone with catalogues and messages in it to your in-tray because that is where you will need to deal with it. If the items relate to cooking and serving food, consider how much you can reasonably store away now in the premium cupboards where they will be easy to access. Of course some things such as a toaster, kettle, sink tidy, drainage rack and spoons by the cooker have to stay out. But can you get rid of most of the rest? If there are items such as post or diaries or wall calendars or school notes or pictures that your children have drawn, get as much of this stuff up on one wall (you can always rotate pictures...) and into drawers as you can. Be ruthless with ornaments. They won't help and will only attract dirt. This is a room that needs to be as clean as possible most of the time. Personally, I am not a fan of open shelves, or magnetic knife racks or mug racks. They collect dirt and grease and don't leave things clean and ready to use. A fruit bowl some way from the cooker is worth having though, so that it ripens properly and you eat your five a day. If you have a table in your kitchen, clear it completely now (except for perhaps the fruit bowl) using the same principle as the surfaces. And if you open the post here, set up a paper bin and an in-tray that you can carry to your office, wherever that is. Go through the fridge and throw out anything you find yourself not using or which is past its sell-by date. If you have a problem with 'wasting' food in this way, remember that putting bad food containing mould or bacteria into your body or your partner's body is not really worth it. Forgive yourself, throw it out and move on.

Planning with a family

Many families use the kitchen as 'checkpoint central' when it comes to organising school activities and arranging lifts. Formalise this process with a calendar and a notice board for school letters and numbers for babysitters, etc. Don't forget to keep a drawer nearby with pens, envelopes, string, plasters, scissors, tape, stamps or whatever else you find yourself routinely needing. If your kids do their homework at the kitchen table consider the sort of stationery it may be useful to store here too. Extra felt-tips? Extra pens? Glue? Rulers, etc? If you spend a lot of time making packed lunches, consider setting up a workstation for this near the fridge. Put the breadbin here and your sandwich bags, plus a chopping board and store the lunchboxes and sweets and drinks you include nearby. Anything to make the job easier!

Common pitfalls

It is likely that you will need to tackle the kitchen in several sessions unless you have the luxury of an uninterrupted day or more to do it. Beware of pulling everything out and letting yourself get overwhelmed. If you do decide to do it all in one day, try to enlist help and keep the pace up. Don't let yourself get too sidetracked by cleaning, and make a list of any items you will need to make your storage more tidy and effective as you go. Did you discover that your drainage rack was inadequate, for example? Or your breadbin rusty? Your bin broken? Or perhaps that you have nowhere to put biscuits? Get the items you need as soon as you can and move things into them, putting them back in the correct zone. The idea is to create a working system as soon as possible. If the process inspires you to deep clean or to repaint, save that until the clearing process is over and the way you function in the kitchen is well established. One of the fatal mistakes that people make is not to finish the job in hand but to start another 'whilst I'm there'. This is a way of avoiding completion and it isn't as efficient as you may think, as you will tend to run out of steam.

Lastly, the kitchen is usually the first dumping ground for shopping and not everything is a food item that will be put away immediately. Beware of allowing things to sit in the kitchen because you haven't decided on a place for them. Avoid this at all costs.

Laundry

Have a think about where you do this, and how often. Is there a way of making the system you use to collect dirty clothes, and the way you deal with them when they are washed, more efficient? Could you put a laundry basket in the bathroom and encourage everyone to use it so that you don't need to go round all the rooms? Could you site the washer and dryer somewhere outside your kitchen/ diner so that you have more room for cooking and social- ising? And do you need a dryer? Are you littering the house with wet washing on a regular basis? Could you fold the clothes neatly as they come out of the dryer so that you don't need to iron most of them? Where do you store the things to be ironed? Is it near where you will do the ironing? Do you put them straight in the wardrobe afterwards? Find a way of placing things that will make it easy for you to deal with them as you go and cause you the least inconvenience.

A clear kitchen

You know what this final stage is. Sit in your kitchen, have a cup of tea (or a large gin and tonic) and admire it! Breathe in! Feel good! Capture this image. You will need it whenever you need to tidy again and you will need it when you hit those little log jams that occur because your system just wants a tweak. And you know what I will say next. Now that you have a place for everything, keep putting it away as you go. Cleaning will be so much easier. Think about how often and when you will do the washing-up, and when you will do the drying-up and putting away (if you don't have a dishwasher). Perhaps a little every time you are waiting for the kettle to boil?

Chapter ten

Living spaces

The sitting room

This is a really important room in your house. It is the place where you relax and reward yourself at the end of a hard day and the one which is your 'public face' for visitors. Is it also the space where you race around, stuffing things under cushions and behind the sofa, when someone calls unexpectedly? There has to be a more peaceful way to live!

First you need to decide whether your space is formal (i.e. you have some sort of 'den' as well for 'vegging out' in) or whether it has to fulfil all the relaxation functions in your house for yourself and whoever lives with you. If it is formal, you can afford to make it a 'stiffer' space and worry far more about aesthetics. I'm guessing it's the latter though and you need to find a way for this room to fulfil multiple functions.

First check that the sofa and television are really where you want them to be. Do the sofas take advantage of where the best light comes in? Is the television screen obscured by sunlight sometimes? Is there a clear path (or possible clear path) through from the door to the French doors into the garden, etc? If you are confident that the major pieces of furniture in the room are in the right places you can begin.

How to start

As before, we are going to start with a pen and paper. Get yours and list all the tasks carried out in this room: watching television, knitting, reading, chatting, playing computer games, surfing the net, serving tea/drinks, dancing? Band practice? Regular meetings held here, such as a book club? Include in this list any functions that the room doesn't currently fulfil but to which you aspire. Home office areas are dealt with in separate chapters.

Think about where you will be in the space when you do each of these things. Where is the quiet spot to read for instance? Does it take advantage of the light? Does it have a suitable lamp nearby to make it light enough if you are reading in the evening?

Start clearing out as usual in one corner. Pick up the first item and make a decision based on the usual four questions:

1 Do I need and regularly use this? And when?
2 Where do I tend to use it and how often?
3 Do I love it and does it enhance my life?
4 Do I have to store it for some reason?

If the answer to any of these questions is yes, remember to check by thinking about exactly when, specifically, the item will be used, and whether this makes sense.

(*I need that jar. I'm going to make bath oil...* When?
*Well I used to make my own bath oil, but I don't tend to
any more... And I've got loads from last Christmas. Oh
it's such a nice useful-looking jar! Can't I keep it?* No, not
unless you have a specific use on a specific occasion for
it... *Can I store my pulses in it and use it as a display item
on my kitchen shelves.* Yes. *Can I save it until I buy some
mung beans next week?* Yes. *Can I decide not to do that
with it, but keep it just in case I get round to making bath
oil?* No. *I hate you, you know that?* Yup! You get the
idea... By the way, I still have to do this dialogue with
myself sometimes. And you can hate me too if you like...)

Then you have to decide where it belongs. It may be
used somewhere else (in which case move it to that room
immediately, to deal with when you are either organising
or maintaining that room) or it may belong in your sitting
room but just not in that place. Place items where they will
be used. If an object needs to be stored, using the second
question, think carefully about which of your newly
organised storage spaces you are going to put it into and
why. For instance, if you find your walking shoes behind
the sofa and have decided that all frequently used shoes
are to be kept in the hallway, then put them in the hallway,
but if they are your patent leather evening shoes then they
need to go into the wardrobe with all the other seldom-
used items.

What you will do with items that don't achieve a 'yes'
to any of these questions is (in order of preference...):

- Throw them away.
- Recycle them.
- Donate them to charity.
- Give them to someone you know.

Start filling bin bags for each of these categories and, as before, put them in the car at the end of the session so that you will get rid of them at the earliest opportunity. Pick up the next item and make a decision, and then the next and the next. Do not skip items to decide on later because as we know, that way madness lies... Work your way around the walls, clearing cupboards and drawers as you go as well as surfaces, unless any one item is so large that it has to be tackled separately, in which case it should be done first in a dedicated session. You should be producing a visible 'wake' of order. You may end up with a big pile of electronic gear by the TV that you are going to have to decide how to store, if you don't already have a conveniently 'out-of-sight' designated place near it. Finally, clear the coffee table and any piles on the floor around it.

■ Special categories

- *Instruments*: Do you play music in your living room? If it's a small space consider hanging your guitars or bagpipes, or whatever, securely on the wall until you need them, with some sort of storage for your music or your music stand nearby.
- *Books*: Decide on criteria for keeping or ditching these. You may want to have a shelf just for books you

haven't read yet, so that you can put your hand straight on one as you rush to leave the house for a long train journey. There are some reference books it's worth keeping, and if you have the luxury of lots of space then you may want to hang on to all of them, otherwise it has to be just the ones you think you will definitely refer to or read again. Decisions on lots of items of the same type are much easier if you decide on a 'policy' in advance, so think about one for your books now, if you need to.

- *Children's toys*: Have a storage unit or cupboard so that your children can put these away in the living room and request that they do this at the end of the day ... *every day!* There is no reason why you have to live with their chaos. It's your living room too.

- *Crafts*: Do you have a hobby such as knitting or cross stitch? Do you have a place or a workbag where you can store all the things you need to do this activity near your favourite armchair?

- Are there enough coffee tables or places to put a drink down? Are the pictures inspiring and do they go with the room's general colour scheme? Is there somewhere you can place fresh flowers and are your houseplants happy where they are? Would it be nice to frame a number of family photos in the same colour of frame and group them for display? If you have an open fire or woodstove is there enough space and the proper receptacles to store everything you need to keep the fire going?

You will need to list and find answers to all of the above questions (and any others) that apply to you and put the solutions in place (with a shopping trip for storage items or a trip to the dump with the extra rubbish you've thrown out) before you can consider the room finished and the job done.

Dining room

Dining rooms suffer for being one of the first places that collect junk and articles that you don't know where else to store. You know how to clear this area now and your best dinner service and crystal or silver can be stored here and hopefully be on display too. Make this a peaceful, ordered space where you can relax and eat. Try not to store anything else in the dining room unless the space doubles in use for something else, such as dressmaking, for instance. In this case make sure that there are enough cupboards to put all the dressmaking materials away and completely out of sight (perhaps in a storage trolley or behind a screen). If it's a quiet area for homework, then stock a drawer full of useful stationery in your dining room too to make this easier.

Patio

This can be a really fun area to clear. Close your eyes for a moment and imagine yourself here on an ideal day in summer. What are you doing? Having a barbecue? Growing strawberries in container pots? Tending plants? Lounging on a chair with a long cool drink in the shade of an umbrella? Clear systematically, making decisions as you go and removing any item that doesn't support your vision. Take account of where and when the sunlight falls on the patio and arrange your seating accordingly. Remove the stuff that's not needed as soon as possible. Arrange the things you have decided to keep according to your fantasy about how you wish to use the space. And what else do you need? Fairy lights? A table? Some fragrant plants? Make it possible for you to use this area as you first intended and find somewhere out of sight to put all the things you decide you have to keep.

Conservatory

Treat your conservatory like a second sitting or dining room depending on how you and your family use the room.

Den

Make this space a comfortable version of your living room and easy to clean, but don't fall into the trap of thinking that it has to be untidy to be informal. A comfortable space also means easy to use, and a place in which it is hard to find or access things is not comfortable.

Hallway

This is often the first 'dumping ground' in a house and sometimes the clutter that you bring in never makes it beyond this space! The most important thing your hallway does is enable you to transition between home and the outside world. It stores items such as coats and shoes that you need when you're outside, but it should also have a mirror so that you're ready to face the outside world, and a table or shelf where you can put things such as train tickets or letters to post for when you go out. As you come in, you need a place to drop all those things that you don't need for your home life, such as keys and umbrellas, etc. It is not a space in which extraneous items should live except for the very short term, e.g. before it gets taken to the charity shop.

The hall is the gateway to your home. Keep it clear! Is it full of items waiting for you to do things with? Then do them. Don't let this be a place of unfulfilled decisions. You won't feel great about yourself, if the first thing you see when you walk in the door is a pile of things to remind you of what you said you'd do and haven't yet. Enlist some help and get those things done. If you have a really large household, limit everyone to two pairs of shoes and two coats on one peg – that should keep it tidy. Keep your keys on a hook and put them there as soon as you walk in the door. That way you will always know where they are. Don't let things gather in the hall; clear shopping and school bags as you go. Make decisions on new items as to where they really belong immediately. The same goes for the porch. (You thought I'd forget about the junk you have in the porch, didn't you...) Clear systematically as always and create these 'transition zones' now. Get rid of anything that doesn't belong here. Let energy flow freely into your home. You can make it a place that makes you sigh contentedly as you come in and close the front door on the outside world.

Maintenance

Put every item you touch back in its correct zone. First time. Get others to do the same. If it has a logical place to live then they are far more likely to do this.

A special note on smaller spaces

If you are living in a studio flat or a room in a shared house, many of the principles in the preceding chapters will be useful to you. The crucial thing to remember is that this one main room is where you will spend even more of your time than if you had many rooms in a house to use. Therefore, it has to work even harder to provide a calming and supportive place for you to live and study or work, and socialise in. It is even more important that you are ruthless in applying the rules in this book, and there are some additional tricks in this section for you to consider.

Start by getting rid of anything that you don't use or need, and storing anything that you will not need in the next year or so in a separate space if you can. As you start to create zones (and by the way, in a small space, this will make it feel much less chaotic) consider how much you could do to make items of furniture double up in their function. A bed that can be folded away into the wall or become a sofa is invaluable. A storage chest for your pillows and duvet in the daytime, which also provides extra seating, is very useful. A chest of drawers, with the addition of a large mirror on the wall above it, could serve as a dressing table as well as reflecting more light into the room. It can be tempting to have no curtains, but blinds, which take up less space, are a really flexible way of adjusting the level of privacy and light and are generally well worth having.

I think it has to be acknowledged that living in this way is a compromise and will take more effort than you may have to expend in a house. This is because zones will overlap and change function from day to night, etc., and you will need to prepare them or clear them up as you go, if you want to maintain order. As you will be spending so much time in this room, I think it is really worthwhile striving to make it visually clean and clear. At least make it so that, if you wish to put things away, you can do so without feeling that the space still looks chaotic even though you have just tidied up. Otherwise tidying up is going to feel like a thankless task and completely unsatisfying. It will make cleaning much easier if you do that, too.

In a larger space, it is often okay to have magazines, DVDs and other items on display, and you can do that without making it seem cluttered. In this case, however, I think having opaque storage boxes for these and other items, so that they can be stored out of sight, is much more crucial to creating a serene look. DVD covers are designed to grab your attention on the shelf in order to get you to buy them. That is fine whilst they are in the shop, but you don't need them to do that in your small living space. I would suggest that you only leave out things such as the phone or lamps or anything that would be ridiculous to put away in a drawer. If things are going to live on display, they should really have to work to justify the space they take up, both functionally and visually.

I think it is really worth investing, if you can afford it, in some stylish storage options that really fit the space well, and other visual tricks. It is a fallacy to think that, because you live in a small space, planning and investing in it, the way you would with a house, isn't worthwhile. In many ways small spaces are far less forgiving.

Consider using:

- Storage cabinets that make use of awkward corners.
- Coordinating colours and having a limited colour palette. This can make the room seem larger as you are not breaking up the space with boundaries of contrasting colour.
- Light fresh colours, such as cream, white or pale blue, on the walls. The latter, which is 'cooler' in tone will seem to recede.

- Storage boxes that are ornamental and provide some sort of coordinated display.
- Opaque rather than transparent containers so that you can't see what is inside them ... this just adds to the visual 'noise' otherwise.
- Well-chosen ornaments or accessories that go with one strong theme or accent colour that predominates the room.
- Sturdy shelves so that you can get some of your items up away from valuable floor space.
- Walls to hang things, such as musical instruments, so that they are accessible but function as display items for the rest of the time.
- A screen to hide your desk, if the thought of work disturbs you in the evenings when you are winding down.

These are options that are all worth investigating. Items made of good-quality materials or whose design is pleasing will do much to make your space seem luxurious. If you have created clean lines in much of the space, then tactile and well-coordinated scatter cushions or a really attractive rug will add to the ambience without making the room seem more chaotic, but it is best to go with one big 'statement' with items in this category rather than lots of little ones. Don't forget accessories such as flowers (even if they are from the nearest hedge) or a really enticing fruit bowl. In a single-room living space, it can feel luxurious and fresh to have these items on display. Lastly, if you like 'atmospheric' or 'cosy' lighting, investing in a few small lamps (three is an ideal number), or even fairy lights, can transform the feel of a room. Remember that in the evening, what you light up is seen and what you don't 'disappears'. So it can make a living space look cosier if the sofa area is lit but the kitchen area is dark. Make sure your task lighting, such as for your kitchen or your desk, is adequate too.

Put as much away as possible and leave as many clear surfaces as possible. Look at how you use the space (and what you'd like to use it for) and make sure that these functions are well catered for in your zone system. If you forget one of these, say getting dressed in the morning, or what you will do with the laundry, chances are you will find that you create a mess with this task regularly that clutters up the space for the rest of the day.

Living well in a small space takes discipline! It goes without saying that having reassessed and organised your room, the most important habit to develop is the one of putting things back in their correct places as you go. Once it is visually pleasing, however, you will be far more likely to do this automatically. So do a bit of forward planning, invest in a few nice pieces, and give yourself a fighting chance.

Chapter eleven
The home office part 1

This is a major section of the book as people are increasingly working part-time from home or running their own businesses from home. Being organised helps if you are a student too, or if you have several 'hats' or roles in your life, all of which need to be coordinated out of the same home office. It is the one space for which I get the most requests for help. This section is comprehensive enough to cover the needs of those who work from home in a number of roles, but the methodology applies to everyone. If this is a place where you want to create more order, I recommend that you read the whole chapter and find out how much of the system here is useful to you.

The real issue

There are two main issues for anyone organising their home office. One is the ease in which things are arranged so that they can be accessed and used, and the other is the question of how to remember and prioritise tasks so that they get done in a timely fashion. It is this last one that causes people most worry (unless their office tasks are very simple to remember) and which can cause panic if they try to put anything away. Most often, when someone asks for help in organising their home office, this is what they are actually most concerned about, and so this chapter is designed to address that issue. The next chapter deals with the organising of the space.

Commonly, the most important things you need to attend to at work or in life are the ones that have no visual reminder at all, and which cannot be accomplished in a single day or work session. I am thinking of the forward planning that you may need to do, and all the tasks that arise as a result of that, or of deciding what your long-term goals are, and working steadily towards them. These important but nebulous tasks are the easiest to forget about or procrastinate over. But long-term goals may not be what you are most concerned about. You may also find that you chronically procrastinate on the small tasks too. This chapter is going to be an exception to the others and address the issue of time and prioritising to some degree as well as the organising of things, because in a home office, these two are very closely linked.

You may have been giving yourself a hard time over all of the above, without understanding that your physical systems aren't making it easy for you to focus properly, either on long-range goals, or the everyday tasks themselves. Studies done in the 1990s showed that productivity improved an average of 20 per cent when an office was pleasant to work in and well organised. I think knowing this is important if you expect yourself to work hard. In addition, wouldn't it just feel so much nicer to work from a calmer space?

What to expect in this chapter

If your office is a real mess or you have a sinking feeling when you work in it that things are 'getting lost' in the system, then reorganising your office will be a major task, and one that takes a serious amount of commitment from you to accomplish. As usual we are going to use the toothbrush principles of grouping by function, zoning, and completion to deal with the problem, but since we are also dealing with your work (which may take the form of ideas) and not just physical 'stuff', the system we use has to take account of this. For this reason it is a little more complex. I suggest that you start by reading this chapter all the way through in order to get a feel for what we are going to do.

How this home office system evolved

When I first started out working from home, I was largely reactive and this made organising my office space relatively easy. If something came in (in those days a letter or phone call) I would simply put it in my in-tray and set some time aside in the week to deal with everything there so that it didn't get too full. Knowing what I had to do was easy, knowing when it was building up was easy, and so too was knowing when I had finished. There was a visual cue for all of these things and it was the state of my in-tray. I was young then and was actually carrying a lot of other tasks and schedules in my head but my memory was so good and it was so effortless that I didn't realise it. One of the things that changed over the years was that I developed lots of other 'roles' and that the volume of my administration tasks grew. And I hate to admit it but I got older. In the past few years as a singer, I have juggled developing my own voice and technique with teaching workshops in various settings plus teaching private pupils, doing concerts, doing occasional sessions for other people, tour managing myself and administrating my own catalogue as a songwriter, doing most of the legal work required for all these situations and writing this book. As my work has got more complicated and diverse, and my memory has got less efficient, I have had to evolve concrete systems that deal with all those extra aspects of what I need to do so that none of them gets neglected and so that I 'work smart' wherever possible.

These days I use five tools to keep me on track. Two in-trays (one real and one virtual), a diary, a calendar and a day book. My desk is clear virtually all the time, but tasks and things hardly ever get forgotten or lost. And I don't generally miss deadlines. If your fear is that putting things away will mean that you lose track of what you have to do, don't worry. There is a system which I will outline here that (providing you follow it properly) will help you to feel much more focused, effective and in control.

Your initial assessment

Have a walk round your workspace and think about how your current 'if I see it I will do it' system is working for you (if that's the one you use). Are you caught up? Are there piles of paper all over the place that you daren't disturb in case you lose something? Have you really done all those little things that you said you would? Or if you went through those piles of stuff would you find a CD waiting to be returned to someone, or a sample of your work that you meant to send out to that interesting contact you met at a meeting a month ago? Or possibly a library book you meant to return? Or a course that you saw advertised that you meant to enquire about? Perhaps, you would say to me: 'Ah, but I have done all the important things. I have done all the major work that needed doing...' Perhaps you have written and given a series of lectures or organised a workshop or done your year's accounts, or some other major task or series of tasks. But when was the last time you looked at what you earn over-all and how many hours it takes you to earn that amount? When was the last time you looked at how you want your business to grow and where you want it to be in five years, and at what you will do now to get it there? When did you last look at what your dreams are and how you are going to finance them? A good system will help you to do these things too.

If the thought of doing something about those larger issues scares you, what is it that feels uncomfortable? What are the things or people that perennially trip you up, and what you can do about them? When did you last set time aside to ask yourself how you would like to grow as a person and what skills you would like to develop, either to create a new income stream, or to make you feel more fulfilled? When did you last plan your days off or your holiday time properly? You may be staying on top of your work, but do you really want to be in the same place in five years' time? And what is your quality of life? Are there problems that constantly trip you up but which you are ignoring? Do you want to raise the money for a really big purchase or a really spectacular holiday or to celebrate a milestone anniversary? If so, how are you going to make that happen? These are difficult things to ask yourself, but you will really benefit if you do. Take a moment to answer some of these questions for yourself, if they are important to you, with a pen and paper.

You are now holding a list of the really important larger issues for you that can get lost even when the 'nuts and bolts' work is getting done. You can help yourself by realising that you need the time, and a system, to help you think about them regularly, and to ground them into definite plans. Your office is the place to do that. It is a representation in physical space of the clarity of your plan-ning process, and it will mirror the quality of that process, as it currently exists in you, very faithfully. Your office can be an alchemical place. It can be the place in your life where your dreams are made concrete and where they can start to become reality – or not!

How to get started

What is your motivation for organising your office? My guess is that you don't feel in control. I'd guess that this is because you have too much stored in your short-term memory about where things are and what you have to do, which makes you feel tense, and that you have developed a low-grade fear that things are running away from you and that you are missing something vital. This is *not* a problem of not knowing where to put things or not having enough space. This is a problem of not knowing where to put things so that you will remember to do them in the proper order and in a timely fashion. It is not so much how to put things away as to how to put them down and not be worried that you will never remember them again.

How do you want to feel sitting at your desk? How do you want it to look? Clear? Calm? Controlled? Well regulated? Peaceful? Inspirational? Take a minute to think about that and hang on to that vision because you are going to need it to sustain you whilst you create a new system. I would hope that you have done most of the other exercises in this book and haven't skipped to this chapter. This is an advanced project and you will need what you have learned so far, to do what you need to do. If you haven't read the earlier chapters, please go back and do the bathroom exercise in Chapter 2 at the very least. More importantly, try out the habit of keeping your bathroom that way for two weeks to see how you feel, before you even think about tackling your office. With offices, maintenance is an important skill.

■ How to get control of your tasks

This is the first monster to tame. As before, read the entire exercise and see yourself going through it before you make a start.

To do this exercise you will need:

- Three sturdy stackable desk trays. (These will be your in-tray, pending tray and 'to file' tray.)
- If you use a computer and have email, you will need an in-tray and a pending tray within this system. (We will look at how to set this up in a moment.)
- A diary. (This can be electronic if you like but it should be portable and go with you everywhere.)
- A good-quality A5 notebook, preferably spiral bound for ease of use, which will act as your 'day book'. (Again you can develop an electronic version of this if you like once you know how it works.)
- A wall calendar or forward planner (I prefer calendars that give you a box for each day. You will need this amount of room in order to fit all your major appointments and commitments in. A line for each day almost certainly won't be enough.)
- Some large rectangular Post-it® notes. (You will need these for checking in, see pages 175–184).

Yes, you really will need all of these things. And no, we can't start properly until you have got them all. This is an all or nothing system. Please keep going and once you have roughly sorted the physical systems described below, *carry on* and start doing the check-ins. This is really important, otherwise all you will have is a temporarily tidier desk. This chapter has to be read and acted on as a whole, or it won't work at all.

■ Are you 'dire'?

You may already have found, as I did, that when it comes to managing tasks, an easy pattern to fall into is the DIRE system:

D iary

I n-tray

R egular/remembered tasks

E mail

This isn't going to help you to be proactive, nor is it going to help you prioritise important tasks in your working day. The aim with this exercise is to create a rough, but complete, working method that will give you confidence that everything (even the big picture) is being taken care of in timely fashion, and to encourage you to start sorting more systematically as you go. Once that method is properly established in your physical space and you are consistently using it, it can be used to help you start clearing the backlog of paperwork, secure in the knowledge that it isn't going to reappear.

■ The new system

First create the physical system as follows. Please give yourself anything from two to three hours to a whole day to finish this part of the exercise all in one go:

1   Make sure all your appointments and time commitments to yourself (both domestic and business) are in your diary. (You should only have one diary.) Do this for the next four weeks. So if you are planning to shop for a sofa on Saturday, or have a meeting with a new client on Monday, or are planning an early night with a bubble bath on Tuesday, the time should be marked in. Block in your regular work hours, and your regular commitments to others, such as picking up the children from school or dropping them at an after-school class. If you need to pay a bill or contact someone on a certain date, this task should also go in your diary. If you have an ongoing commitment at a particular time in the week, such as a meeting or a class, don't forget to mark all of these in as well.

The reason to do this when you 'already know' that you have these commitments is to give you a truer picture of just where your time goes, and you can't do that if some things aren't written down because they're taken as read. Your diary can do more than just tell you where to be and when. In the long term it can help you to start creating time to do what is truly important to you but only if you use it properly. Update your diary every day; don't let it become out of date.

2 Copy all these appointments on to the calendar or
   forward planner for the month in broad terms and
   block out the time visually with a highlighter pen, or
   several in different colours, for example, yellow for
   family events/time, and blue for work-related travel.
   Do you start to see patterns emerging? Do you
   suddenly see that you have four really heavy-duty
   work days in a row and that you are going to need a
   break on the fifth day? If so, schedule it in. Or do you
   see that you are going to be away from your desk for
   three days in row and that you are really going to have
   to put three hours aside the next day to catch up on
   paperwork? Schedule that in also. Transfer this information back to your diary so that you don't double
   book the time.

   This process is crucial if you don't work orthodox
   office hours or if you work on location, or in several
   different places. When you're self-employed, the panic
   can set in and it is all too easy to have worked 10 days
   straight without noticing, and wonder why you feel a
   bit jaded! If you do work office hours then you can get
   away without doing this step, but it is still a useful way
   of assessing your combined work and domestic 'load'
   and may go some way to explaining why you always
   feel exhausted on a Thursday, for instance. If this is the
   case you can see where to cut back on regular commitments earlier in the week. The reason I suggest you
   do this on a calendar and transfer it back is that the
   diary contains too much detailed information for

you to see the broad sweep of how your time is being taken up over a period of weeks, especially if no two weeks are the same. The calendar provides a good overview.

3 Put all the letters that need an answer, lists, and reminder scraps of paper in your in-tray to deal with later. Put everything that needs filing in the filing tray (or if there is really too much to do this, add another tray or put your filing in a large, well-labelled box to deal with shortly). Now put anything that you can't deal with now because you are waiting for information to come in, or which you don't need until a certain date, such as theatre tickets or train tickets, in the pending tray. When you start to work, it is important that you can pick up each set of items knowing that there is only one type of task to accomplish with them. It will help you to make a start every day, if the items are already sorted and waiting for you. It will also help you to know at a glance what you have to get through. This area will start to look very full just now. Don't panic, because you are going to be setting aside time to deal with this systematically. For once, though, you are looking at a true representation of your backlog.

4 Make a list in the front of your A5 book. *This will be a master tasks list to cover anything that your diary or in-tray doesn't prompt you to do.* It shouldn't be more

than a page long. If it is, it is going to make you feel very stressed indeed... On one side of the page, list all the business things that need doing. On the other side, list all the domestic tasks that need completing. These will generally have a much lower priority. This book is also the place for listing all those long-term projects. Listing them here will mean that they don't have to live on your desk all the time. You will be able to put them away without feeling that 'out of sight is out of mind' and more importantly you can keep track of projects that have no visual reminders at all. You can also use this book to make lists of questions to prepare for important phone calls and to note the answers, and to take to meetings to make notes. Using it in this way will provide a useful record of what was said and promised by you or someone else on a particular date (as you will date these entries) and take even more strain off your memory. Or you can use it to plan new projects, brainstorm or make notes. But never allow yourself to make more than one current 'to do' list at a time.

Usually at this point people merrily write down every task they can think of, even whimsical ones that don't really matter. It is as if they are just 'dumping' ideas on the page. If your planning process has been chaotic, it is likely that you have been using the 'if I can't remember to do it, it's not important' method of filtering. The point is, just because you can write it down, doesn't mean you shouldn't edit your list as you go, otherwise you will scare yourself and end up spending time on a lot of peripheral unimportant things. If your master list is longer than a page, then you will need to prune it. Do this in the following ways:

a) On a separate page, list the six biggest projects (aside from all the regular tasks) that you have going in your life at the moment both at work and at home. Remember your projects may relate to study, finding better work, improving your income, growing your company, clearing your clutter, getting fit, or anything else that is important to you. If any tasks on your list don't relate to moving these forward and are not essential, then ditch them. Cross them off the list now. If you really must, list them on a Post-it® (or series of Post-it®s by category) and put them in the back of the notebook to be rescued when you remember (and if they are important to you, you will remember).

If you have a problem narrowing it down to just six, remember that your brain will focus on a few important things more easily than many (enabling you to reach your initial goals more quickly and get on to the next ones). Remember also that if you analyse the goals that you want to achieve, you will find that they actually need to be accomplished in a certain order of priority. For instance, if you are trying to find your soulmate and also establish yourself in a new field of work, would you be more likely to meet someone who suits you in that field? If so, it may be worth putting the soulmate goal on the back burner.

b) List all the time-sensitive tasks in your diary. So, for instance, if you know you are going to drive to the next town on Friday for a meeting, list all the things you need to buy and all your errands there on a Post-it®, and store it by that date in your diary (of course, schedule in the time to do this on your trip). You can do even more, however. Will your route take you past other places where you could schedule other meetings and errands? Don't forget to book these in, if necessary, as well. Then add them to your Post-it® for that date and cross them off the master list. You don't need to think about these any more until you are ready to go.

c) Schedule phone calls that have to be made on a certain day or at a certain time in your diary. Cross these off the master list too, even though you haven't made them yet. You don't need to be reminded twice (provided you are really in the good habit of checking in with your diary every day) and there is nothing more stressful than constantly skimming a list with tasks on it that you can't tackle yet.

d) Come back to your important projects. Either with pen and paper, or using a Word document with a table of three columns, start a sheet for each project. On each one, start to list all the actions you would need to take in order to move the project towards completion, together with your ideal deadline for each task. If you can do this on a computer, you can re-order them into a proper sequence later, but don't let yourself take too much time over this. Sometimes pen and paper is more freeing and definitely quicker. Take a minute to brain-storm regularly with this sheet, so that you look at all the smaller steps and ideas that are going to get you closer to your desired outcome. You can tick off the tasks as you complete them.

So, for instance, if you are in debt and trying to resolve this, you will head the sheet 'Resolve debt problem' and may have tasks such as: 'Set up meeting with accountant' (or whoever is going to help you), 'Make a list of ways to save money', 'Visit comparison websites for car insurance and other bills', 'Make a budget', 'Research part-time work', 'Get debt coun-selling' and so forth. You want to list the action on one side (or in one column) and note the date by which you want to achieve it in the next, and finally the date that you completed it (once you have done so), in the third. So if, for example, you have requested changes to a contract, then you can note the date on which that request was made, and make a note in your diary as to when to chase up the answer if you haven't heard by then. In the meantime, you can get on with some other aspect of that project (such as researching the infor-mation you will need when it goes ahead) that you can do in the meantime.

You will end up with a sheet for each of your proj-ects. Only two or three of the most immediate tasks from each sheet needs to go on to your master list unless you know that you need to make more progress on that particular project in that week. This will stop you feeling upset when you try to break your 'get book published' goal down into manageable chunks and then get overwhelmed because you generate half a page of useful ideas, all of which feel as though they should have been done yesterday! Alternatively, you may find that you are someone who just needs to look at the project list as a reminder, check the status of that particular goal, and simply do the next thing that will move it on most effectively that day. Check each of these sheets twice a week, or add a task from one of them whenever you cross another task from the same project off your master list using the 'one out, one in' principle.

I recommend having a few clear document folders and storing each project list in a separate one to be placed in your 'Pending' desk tray so that you remember to consult them regularly. If you do this and you spot a related newspaper article or collect a business card or some other resource, you can throw this in the same folder so that it's there when you need it. If I'm planning an event, or preparing for a presentation, or singing at a festival, I do the same thing with everything from the e-tickets to my working notes for that particular event, all in the same folder, which is then easy to grab when I'm packing.

In addition, when I have a routine task that always follows a similar structure (say booking gigs, for example, when there's always a contract, travel and soundcheck to be arranged) then I find it useful to set up a master list or spreadsheet that I can fill in every time. It can be updated as I learn what to check on, and helps to keep me on the ball.

e) Regular tasks, such as walking (if you have a fitness goal) or instrument practice, can either be listed on a separate page (to be consulted at check-in time every day) or scheduled straight into your diary, for example, the gym three times a week.

f) Try to cut back on things that you have volunteered to do for others if you are really so overwhelmed and tend to get behind, yourself. Cancel these if you can, and simply don't take them on at all next time. Think about whether there are any tasks, either regular or one-offs, that you can delegate easily and do so as soon as possible. I know this is difficult because there is usually some element of emotional blackmail involved. It sometimes helps to weigh up how much time, inconvenience and effort the commitment will take and to explain that gently to the person to whom you have made the commitment.

g) Update your lists every day. You will find that some jobs just don't need to be done, or that something else does instead, as time goes on. As you add and cross tasks off the list, you will find that you regularly need to start a fresh page, date it and re-list any unfinished tasks that you still need to do from the old list. It should never be longer than one page.

You should now find that your master list is much more manageable. Rewrite it on a fresh page now, if necessary. If there are tasks that you are constantly avoiding, see the maintenance section below.

5 Next, email, if you use it. This is an amazingly efficient way of organising your emails that I read about years ago; I wish I could remember where! Open your email programme. We are going to create a virtual in-tray system here, which will make it much easier for you to see, at a glance, what is important or urgent and to stay on top of it.

Create an in-tray and a pending tray in your list of folders like this. Firstly decide what these are to be called. Mine are called 'ACTION' and 'PENDING'. If you select 'Local folders', right click (if you are a Mac user, click the 'list of actions for mail' icon), then select 'create a new folder' in your general list and type the @ symbol first: it will automatically list this folder at the top of all the others that you have the power to create. This is important because you want your virtual in-tray to be very easy to see. Create two new files in this way and name them @ACTION and @PENDING. Using capitals also makes them easier to see. They should head up all your other file folders after your inbox, outbox, sent items, deleted items and drafts.

Now go to your inbox and drag any item you still have to deal with into @ACTION. If your inbox is full of thousands of messages, do this for messages received in the last week so that you at least make a start. Drag any item that indicates you are waiting for a reply before you can act into @PENDING. Delete any unwanted emails as you go. If an email contains information that you may need to access again, 'flag' it before you store it so that it will be easy to find it. Drag anything else that is finished with or which doesn't need a reply, but you need to keep, into an appropriate storage file. If you don't have any storage files create a few in order to do this. So you may need ones such as 'personal letters', 'business letters', and specific ones for clients or projects. I also suggest that you start one called 'orders' in which you can file all emails relating to things you have ordered online, password emails, confirmations, and emails relating to bills and so forth that you manage online. Yes I know not all your emails are sorted like this. You will have a backlog that is stored a little erratically, but I don't want you to get bogged down in this. You don't have the time, nor is it that important for the moment.

- Now go back to your inbox. It should be empty (or at least empty of messages from the last week). Your inbox is the equivalent of your doormat, i.e. the place where your post lands. It isn't that helpful to try to deal with it there. That is simply an arrival point.
- Go to your outbox. If you are online it will be empty.
- Go to your sent items folder. This will contain a bunch of sent emails. Sort these as you did the ones in your inbox. If you are finished with the transaction, file the mail in a storage folder. If you are waiting for a

response, drag it to the @PENDING folder. Or if you have promised to act on it drag it to @ACTION.

Do you see a pattern emerging here? All the active folders, in which your email programme does things automatically, are folders that you are going to attempt to clear and leave empty at the beginning and end of every email session. This is because what your programme does is outside your control. Letting it dictate how you work is like letting your Auntie Joan sort your mail for you. She may be well meaning, but if she knows as little about your work as your email programme does, it isn't going to help! It doesn't help you to leave what you need to deal with in your inbox, ready for your next admin session, only to find it clogged up with unsorted incoming mail the second you next log on. That is like leaving your neatly organised in-tray on the doormat, and coming down in the morning to find it flooded with that day's junk mail. What a mess! Suddenly you are overwhelmed because you don't know what to deal with next and you don't even want to start. You need to sort your mail, and put it elsewhere, before you attempt to deal with it.

You will find that the task seems much easier and more achievable if you are only looking at items you've decided to take action on, and which you can deal with immediately. It takes a little getting used to and feels a little pedantic at first, but please try it for a while. If you have a lot of emails waiting in your in-box and you decide to sort them all in one go, you will need to leave roughly one hour per 150 emails to clear them. If you don't have time to sort them all in one go, or even to do all those dated in the last week, then sort all the emails with today's date and yesterday's date using this system, so that you can get on with dealing with what's in your @ACTION folder right now. Do that and experience for yourself how much easier it is when you know you can clear the whole folder. Then tomorrow you will deal with tomorrow's mail plus one more day's worth of backdated emails. This gets easier and easier as you go on obviously, because after a few days you will be dealing with the backlog that is increasingly irrelevant to your current situation and the backlog email will become simple to delete or to store.

So to reiterate: your inbox, outbox, sent items, and drafts folder should be empty at the end of every email session you have and you will need to spend a few minutes every time making sure that this is so. Your @ACTION folder should contain only items you can act on now and intend to deal with. Ideally, this should be empty at the end of every email session too. Your @PENDING folder should contain emails that prompt you about information you are expecting from colleagues. You should update this whenever you receive the reply you are expecting and are able to act on it. In addition, every few days you need to check this folder for items that you need to chase up. This is particularly useful when you are delegating, or working

to an urgent deadline with others. It will make it easy
for you to be 'on the ball'. Any other emails should
either be deleted or filed.

At this point your in-tray and your email in-tray, and your
master list, will be groaning with things to be done. Groaning with all the things that were ignored in your piles of
stuff all over the place. It can be tempting to think that
putting all this stuff in five different piles reduces it to a fifth
of what it was. It doesn't really, does it? It just gives you an
easier way to ignore the volume of what is actually there. If
this is your situation at the end of this initial phase, set up
some serious time, perhaps a day, to clear your two in-trays
and make a start on the tasks on your master list. This is
really important and will stop you feeling overwhelmed.
Keep reading to the end of the chapter for tips on how to
do this and how to cut back on the things that aren't really
that important. Be ruthless and stay focused! Remember,
although it can feel like an achievement to have written the
list or gathered all those items together in your in-tray, it
isn't. That's just the start. That's like putting the teabag into
the cup; you haven't made the tea yet! Please set aside some
serious time to start dealing with the backlog, or you will be
tempted to let the whole thing slide again.

Quick recap on organising the physical system

1   Go through your diary and make sure it has absolutely
    every appointment you've made in it for the next month,
    including personal ones you've made for yourself.

2 Block these commitments out roughly in your calendar and highlight broad categories of time, for example, days away from your desk, days off, days on a course, etc. Use the perspective this gives you to avoid time crunches in advance. Schedule in family time, administration catch-up time and days off when you can see you are going to need them (these are usually the things that get forgotten). Make appointments with yourself or family or colleagues, if necessary, and transfer these plans back to your diary.

3 Make a master list. Use one side of the page for business tasks and the other for domestic. Having both of these on one page will help you see where you can combine them to your advantage. (And, realistically, every parent knows they need to think like this sometimes.) Work out what your top six priorities are and try to make your list reflect this. Ditch anything that is non essential. Move time-specific tasks such as bill paying, posting a birthday card or making a business call to your diary and try to maximise efficiency here by grouping errands logically. Delegate or offload tasks wherever this is sensible. Prune your list to one page.

4 Make project lists. Brainstorm for the steps you will need to take and set up a list with deadlines, which can live in your pending tray for you to consult as you need to. Only two or three of the first of these tasks needs to be listed on your master list as you will keep

adding more from your project list to your master list as you complete them.

5   Put all filing in the filing tray.

6   Put any items you will need later or need to deal with later and your project lists in your 'Pending' tray.

7   Put any item that needs to be dealt with in your 'In-tray'.

8   Write a list of regular daily tasks either in your A5 book or on a piece of paper to be referred to every day.

9   Set up your virtual email 'In-tray' and 'Pending' tray and sort and deal with at least today's and yesterday's email.

10 Schedule in some serious time to deal with the backlog in your filing, physical 'In-tray' and email 'In-tray'. Plough through it as quickly and ruthlessly as possible when you do.

■ The habit on which the entire system depends
Okay, that is the physical system dealt with for the moment. Now, and this should be done straight away, I am going to ask you to do something absolutely crucial and central to this system and to feeling in control. I am going to ask you to commit to *ONE* absolutely essential habit on which this system entirely depends.

Check in with the method described on page 178, each and every morning.

Yes, check in every morning first thing. Alternatively, if you are an 'owl' and are more focused at night, do it last thing before you leave your desk for the day, in which case your subconscious mind will obligingly work on those tasks for you overnight. This is a good policy if you find you are always late in the morning too. Nothing short of a major fire should stop you unless you are away, of course, and have allowed for being away and not checking in. It will only take you 10 minutes or less. I am not saying you have to start the day with administration tasks. I am not saying you have to become a slave to your desk. But feeling in control, in this case, means knowing that you are on top of what needs to be done, and on top of any deadlines. In order not to overload yourself and not to be tempted to try to finish everything at once, you need to be able to do what has to be done that day and then put the task/s down, *confident* that you will pick them up again when you need to. This is especially important if you have lots of roles in completely different fields.

If you find yourself rebelling at this point, I do understand. Perhaps you need to be reminded that you already do a quick mental check on what is important, most days. Otherwise, you might just forget about your responsibilities, drive to the seaside and eat ice cream on the promenade. I certainly would! What you are doing with this habit is making the mental check you already do every day more efficient and more formal. That way, you can make it balanced and make sure that you are on top of everything so that you can be relaxed. It is very tempting to keep working through on one thing and forget other projects whose deadlines then catch you by surprise, or to work hard and forget to do the things that keep you fit and healthy or even fit for, and up to date for, your work.

I find that if I just do the things that are nagging at me, and which I remember:

- I am about 20 per cent less efficient in my planning.
- I pick off the easy tasks, whether they should be done first or not.
- I don't get round to the everyday maintenance stuff such as a proper vocal warm-up or some exercise (and in the long term, missing out on this regularly can really harm the quality of my work).
- I work about 20 per cent less because I lose momentum as I vacillate about what to do next.

I know that particular 20 per cent is where all the long-term important stuff gets done, and not just the knee-jerk tasks, i.e. the ones that others think I should do. That 20 per cent is the breathing space that enables me to shape my own working life and achieve my own ambitions, rather than someone dictating to me. It doesn't always mean working harder and longer either. It can just mean having the perspective to be able to see what is important. This, for me, is the most crucial reason to do it. The way to achieve this 'little and often' balance, that takes account even of those long-term and very important (but not press-ing) goals, is this…

■ How to check in

Get one of those rectangular Post-it® notes. You are going to start writing your list of tasks for today on it. The acronym I use for checking in is:

A

D iary

M asterlist

I n-tray

R egular tasks

E mail

If you don't make this check-in the A1 priority first thing … what you get is MIRED, because these tasks don't go away. They just build up and become confusing if you don't have some way of tackling them systematically. (Okay, I agree, enough of the feeble acronym puns…)

Diary

Check in by looking at your meetings or commitments for the day and the pressing deadline tasks in your diary. Note these essentials on the Post-it®.

Master list

Then, if you are going to have time, put in some tasks (in order of importance!) from your master list. So if you have to meet an urgent deadline by writing a report then put that on the list. Or if (hopefully) you have no urgent deadlines but would earn more if you widened your skill base, then researching courses might be a really important (although not urgent) use of your time. Try to balance your time out so that you touch base with each of the important projects that you have on the go at the moment. Pick a task for each of these that would move it forward, unless, of course, there is a current 'window of opportunity' for one of them, in which case concentrate on maximising that.

In-tray
Schedule some time on your Post-it® to deal with this if you need to.

Regular tasks
After that, put on your Post- it® the things that you have to do to keep yourself healthy or up to speed, such as the gym, your daily walk, special exercises from the physiotherapist or whatever else it is best for you to do every day.

Email
Being regular and up to date with your email replies will give everyone you deal with confidence. Remember to estimate the time you'll need to do this realistically. To cut down on the time it takes, I recommend checking it two to three times a day and closing the programme otherwise.

Write the amount of time you think you'll need by every task and try not to schedule more than four hours' worth.

You may get away with scheduling six hours, if some of this is going to be taken up with well-planned meetings that don't drag on. This is because things always take longer than you think they will and because you will almost certainly be interrupted in your tasks.

■ The benefits of checking in

Now you have a list that properly reflects your commitments to yourself and to others in order of importance. You can get on with it, confident that you will be doing the most important things first and confident that you don't have to worry about getting everything done that day, because you will be doing the same tomorrow and the next day and the next. You will be confident that your mountain of work is being tackled steadily and systematically every day, so you can lose that awful vague feeling that you're not on top of things, because you absolutely know that you are. *If you don't keep your commitment to yourself to check in every day then the system falls apart.* You can't put things down so easily because you don't know when they will be tackled again. Basically, you will have stopped trusting yourself and with good reason!

If you are resisting quantifying your work and taking an overview like this every day, ask yourself why? If you feel that making this kind of regular commitment makes you feel 'owned' by your work, well, is feeling uneasy and 'hunted' when you don't, actually any better? As a friend of mine recently said, 'I'd rather have *actual* anxieties about *actual* things than a general anxiety about something I think I should be doing if only I knew what it was…'. If you don't like the idea of routine then try keeping a time diary for a week or two. Note down how you actually spent your time. You will probably discover that you are much more a creature of habit than you think. Remember that you can arrange for yourself not to check in for a week or more if you know that you are not needed at your desk in that time, if that is what you wish. Or when you check in, you can make sure that what you do today is nothing like what you did yesterday. The idea is simply to be on top of things and to know for sure what you need to do, in the same way that you check your mobile phone for texts or messages regularly. It is simply a way of staying in touch with your workload. Just having a 'to do' list will not give you a big enough perspective to take all your long-term goals into account. It makes what others request of you seem more important than what you have decided you would like to achieve yourself.

Assessing your workload like this can make it seem overwhelming. If you have been kidding yourself about how much you work, by separating it out into different categories in your own mind, it can be disheartening to view it all as a whole. This is only the same strategy as making five piles of stuff instead of using one in-tray though, isn't it? The human mind has a tendency to do this. It is very common to find that people with serious debt problems have no idea how much they owe, because they have spread the amounts out, across several store and credit cards. That makes their debt burden seem lighter than it is, but it doesn't help them to get out of trouble in the long term. My purpose in asking you to look at your workload as a whole is to make it easier for you to see how hard you do actually work, so that you can get some perspective about what is important to you, and take steps to reduce the number of tasks, if necessary.

The other reason to make the commitment to check in with yourself every day is so that you can stop feeling that you have to carry your A5 notebook (which should remain on your desk unless you are taking it to a meeting to make notes), your project files, or even your entire filing system around with you, in order to be sure that you are doing what most needs to be done.

■ Working with your list

Let's get back to your Post-it® list. Keep it with you to refer to all day and tackle everything on it, crossing things off as you go. (I tend to use Post-it®s, because they are easy to keep on your desk or in your diary if you are going out, and harder to drop or lose.) I suggest that you maximise your mental efficiency by doing one thing at a time. I think the idea of multi-tasking is largely a myth (unless you are waiting for something that doesn't need a chunk of your attention to get done, such as the washing, or the dish-washer). So, if you pick something up, stick with it. Don't get distracted. If it reminds you of another task you need to do, then write it on your Post-it®, at the bottom so that you can add it to your master list, to deal with another time and then forget it. If you are someone who has ideas that strike you all the time whilst you are out, then stick an extra Post-it® by your check-in Post-it® so that you can note things down and transfer the ideas to the correct project or shopping list or to your master list as appropriate.

Deal with whatever you started until it is finished and don't try to do anything else in the meantime. If you're one of those people who tends to think of all the reasons why you can't get a job done and it seems like an insoluble problem, think of three solutions, however wacky, to break the block in your thinking. Think of one way in which you can move the task forward even if you don't have the answer – such as asking someone that you think does have an answer. Don't allow yourself to get stuck. Perhaps you have asked yourself to do too much at once. Break the task down if you can and do the first step, however small, listing the others on your master or your project list. Sometimes, taking the first really easy baby step can break the deadlock and make the whole answer more obvious.

Lastly, as I said earlier, if you are a night owl and work better at night, it can be useful to do your check-in for the next day, the night before. Make your list and let your subconscious mind work on it overnight. This is also useful if you have an early train or plane to catch and need to make a couple of phone calls or drop something off on the way out or beforehand. In that case, make a list that details very clearly, what you have to do before you get on the train and what you will need to do later in the day. This will save you having to think too hard. It always makes me feel peaceful and virtuous, even if I am groggy.

(Yes, feeling virtuous is allowed if it helps me get the job done ... even if it is pure delusion!)

Having organised the basic system, here are some ways to maximise your efficiency as you start to work through your tasks.

Dealing with your in-tray

When the post comes in, sort it out over the bin (or the recycling box). Throw away anything that you aren't going to need immediately. This includes time-wasting stuff such as catalogues that you aren't really going to order from, all junk mail including requests from charities (unless they are from ones to which you regularly donate), and all envelopes (unless they are reply envelopes). Try not to succumb to the 'ooh that's interesting' thought. Anything you don't ditch now is only going to add to your load. Be ruthless. You can always retrieve the article from the recycling if it really haunts you and that is a good test. (If you don't recycle, this is a good reason to start ... quite apart from all the obvious ones, of course!) Put the rest of the post to deal with in your in-tray.

When you have scheduled time to deal with what's in your in-tray, use the golden 'completion' rule. Pick up the first piece of paper on the pile. Deal with it. If you can't finish the task required, do all that you can to move it forward and then put it where you will be reminded to finish the task. (For instance, if you are writing to someone to request more information regarding an offer their letter contains, then put a copy of your reply with the letter in the pending tray to check on next week.) Don't put it down until you have. Pick up the next piece of paper on the pile. Deal with it. And so on until you get to the bottom of the tray. Unless there is something in there that has a really important and imminent time deadline on it, do not sift through your in-tray skipping from task to task, never dealing with anything properly, or only dealing with what you feel like. All you will be doing is making your in-tray feel more chaotic and leaving all the hard stuff for yourself to do later (and if you don't feel like doing it now, when are you going to feel enthusiastic about it?) When you have got to the bottom of the tray you will feel great!

If you do this regularly when there are only a few items in there and not piles and piles of stuff, you will feel confident that everything gets dealt with in a timely fashion and that nothing is getting lost. Be ruthless and shelve anything that you don't really need to do. Sift through your pending tray once a week and shift anything that needs dealing with to your in-tray to be dealt with at your next administration session. Use this principle with your email in-tray and pending tray too.

Some reminders

Hopefully you won't have scheduled in too much, and will be able to finish all the items on your daily check-in list without feeling too rushed or fatigued, but if you don't, then you can always add the unfinished task/s to tomorrow's list. This doesn't indicate failure at all. If a time-management specialist were overlooking your day, they'd probably tell you that you dealt with other urgent and unexpected things that weren't on your list in the first place, but which were more practical to deal with just then.

As you go along:

- Don't forget to cross items that you have done from your daily to-do list off in your A5 book too, and to use that action to prompt you to consult your project lists on what to do next, if you use these.
- Clear your in-tray regularly (oh the joy of seeing the bottom of it!) Anything really urgent in it should have a reminder on your master list or in your diary too so that it doesn't get lost under everything else.
- Keep updating your master list as you realise what needs to be done. Writing things down here is very important.
- You can use your diary to prompt you too. So if you are writing to someone you suspect won't reply without an extra nudge, put a note in your diary by the appropriate date to give them a call or to chase them up when you send the letter off. You are aiming not to rely on your memory at all.
- And go through your pending trays (both real and virtual) once a week so that you prompt people who haven't got back to you, or chase up on things you've ordered that haven't arrived yet, or get round to less pressing tasks and don't let them fall between the cracks.
- File as soon as the filing tray gets full.

A trial period

Make a firm commitment to do all this for two weeks in order to really test it out. It will tell you lots about how you are scheduling your time. Are you over committed? Does seeing what you really have to do every day, and how long it takes to accomplish it, help you to say 'no' a little more often? What people often find to their chagrin is that their administration and planning tasks actually take up about double the amount of time that they thought, and that they haven't been leaving enough time to finish them. This often causes a slowly accumulating backlog that leaves them feeling out of control. If this is you, keep reading for tips on how to cut things down to size.

At the end of the trial time you have committed to, you should be feeling that you have a system you can rely on that encompasses everything important that you need to do. It should also help you to get it done in time and to see what can easily be ditched. You may not like having to spend that amount of time on administration, but unless you honestly acknowledge to yourself how much time it actually takes, you can't take concrete steps to reduce it.

How has the system worked after the trial period?

Now let's look at how you have been getting on, whether this is working for you and what needs fine-tuning (because it will!) What have you noticed about your patterns? Did you prioritise the easy-to-do but less important tasks? Especially the domestic ones? If you did, I would guess that you lost confidence a little bit and went back to feeling tense. With this system you are making a promise to yourself to check what is important to you to achieve every day and to do it in order of importance, if at all possible. Did you skip three or four or five days? Wasn't it scary to go back to your desk and didn't it get harder and harder as time went on? The monster 'chaos' feels like it is winning more and more territory the longer you leave your desk unattended (unless it's planned as I said before…). Did you check in mid afternoon instead of first thing and discover that you hadn't been doing what was important at all, but had been 'cherry picking'? Have you let yourself put post down in random places rather than sorting it correctly first time?

Let's analyse the backlog and how to stop it appearing again:

■ Look at your in-tray
How effectively do you sort what goes into it and deal with what's in there? Did you deal with each thing you picked up until it was finished, or did you abandon it and put it back in the in-tray halfway through? Did you stop using the in-tray efficiently and start making little piles of more urgent stuff to deal with everywhere else (in effect creating five in-trays, all of which you had to keep track of?) Did you do this because you had filled it up and not scheduled enough time to simply get on top of what was in there in the first place? *No amount of organising your tasks can stop you sliding into chaos if you don't actually*

spend enough time doing the tasks needed. If you are resisting this, why is that? Can you get some help? Or can you face more squarely the amount that you need to do regularly, in order to stay on top of things?

■ Look at your email

Did you keep sorting your email as described, religiously every day? If not I'd guess your email looks really messy now. Spend a bit of time sorting it out. Are you adding to your email burden by sending or forwarding unnecessary messages? Perhaps you could make it a rule only to answer personal messages in the evenings and have a special in-tray in which you store them until you are ready. Your emails are likely to increase rather than otherwise. If you can't type at a reasonable pace, think very seriously about biting the bullet and doing an intensive touch-typing course. You can buy them on the web. I sacrificed one May bank holiday to do one and it was the best thing I ever did.

■ Look at your master list

What is continually not getting attended to on the work side of the list? How important is it? Could you delegate it or afford to pay someone else to do it for you? Is there a whole raft or category of tasks that you could delegate to someone else? If you manage a band, for instance, and hate cold calling to get gigs, would it be more effective to get an agent even though you would have to pay them a percentage? Would your time be better spent instead on a different area entirely? You are not doing yourself any favours if you are avoiding a whole set of tasks that you think you 'should' do but which take ages and which you don't attend to properly. And letting yourself off the hook may free you up to make money in other ways, which you do enjoy.

■ Lastly, look at your diary

When you mark your regular work hours and your regular leisure commitments and regular tasks in your diary, how does it look? There probably isn't as much time as you thought, is there? When you add in travel and preparation time for your appointments it starts to look much more crowded, but this is the amount of time that these appointments actually cost you. Include the time you spend watching television programmes that you're hooked on and there isn't much left. When you realise how precious the unallocated time is, and how tired you are after doing all the things in your diary that are really important, does that make it a little easier to say no to activities that don't really fulfil you?

If you haven't actually sat down and scheduled in the time it takes you to do what you actually need to accomplish in a week, including all the obvious regular and mundane tasks, like washing-up or the laundry, you can unconsciously feel that you don't get enough done and don't do it fast enough. It is as important to have *as accurate* an account of how you spend your time, as it is for you to know how you spend your money. Maybe even more so. We can all find ways to earn more money, but none of us can ever earn more time. No one, however rich or powerful, has more than 24 hours in a day or seven days in a week. If yours is not being spent accomplishing your dreams or doing what is important to you (such as having good quality family time), and you are not being really ruthless in carving pockets of time into your schedule where these things can actually happen, remember that you will never get that time back. This is the best reason to be organised in the space where you, essentially, plan your life!

Look at what went wrong and make an effort to fix it (reading all of this section again if you need to) and to recommit to any of the good habits that lapsed. If necessary, get some help. Maybe you could schedule in some time where you can get a friend to be your PA for the day or the afternoon. You could do this as a straight swap if they need help being organised too. As you organise the tasks for them to do, you just may find yourself being clearer about what you need to get on with yourself, and you can make an appointment with yourself to tackle those difficult tasks (you know, the ones you've been avoiding…) whilst they are there. Once you have done this and feel you have a handle on it, we can look at the question of the physical space.

Chapter twelve
The home office part 2

Dealing with the physical space

Now we are going to start tidying your office, but slowly. The way your office looked was not half as important as making sure that it was running smoothly, so I have left this until last.

It is going to sound obvious, but before we sort anything out, take a look at where you have put your desk. Is it a good place to work? Does its position take advantage of the natural light in the room? Do you have your back to the door when you sit at it? Does that make you feel jumpy? If it is in a room that is used for something else, is it in a quiet place? Take a moment to consider whether you want to move it and where it may best be placed. You are going to spend many, many hours at your desk. Put it where you are going to feel most comfortable and where you think you will work well. Its location should also be aesthetically pleasing to you. In addition, you should have enough plug points and phone cables, etc., to make working here practical. The principle here is to make the space as easy for you to work in as possible so that you are encouraged to sit down at your desk regularly and get on with things. Sitting at your desk should feel like a pleasure (to your senses anyway, even if the thought of work isn't!) So, do that now and think about the way in which you use it. I like to compare my desk to a luxury car. It should feel comfortable with all the controls at my fingertips. Similarly with yours, all the tools and supplies you commonly use should be nearest to you and easy to access, and there should be plenty of clear space for you to spread your current project out in. This is our end goal and it's tempting to achieve this immediately by clearing away all the detritus on your desk and shoving it away in a drawer or a box. But if you did that, you know by now that it wouldn't stay that way. We are going to have to work more systematically than that.

Getting started

As usual you are going to work from the outside in and to use the toothbrush principle of zoning to make it easier to access all the items you need for any task you're doing, and to make completion easier and automatic. Start allocating time to clear the storage spaces furthest away from your desk. Set aside an hour or so to do this whenever you can.

Think of yourself as being the queen of a hive. You live in the centre. In fact, wherever you are defines the centre. Any area that is close to you is a premium space. It has to earn its keep by housing things that you need most of the time. Things that you need less frequently can afford to be stored further away, because you won't be spending the time to get up to get them, as often. It doesn't make sense to put your end-of-year accounts in the top drawer of your desk when you only look at them once a year, and your stapler (which you use every day) on a cabinet on the other side of the room... We are going to make sure that every item is placed logically in terms of how you use it, and how often. To make sure we can do this, we will start with the areas furthest away from your desk. This means that as we get closer to it, we will have well-organised spaces in which to 'demote' and put away the things that you don't need that often, leaving us with just the important items to organise close to where you sit.

■ Clearing storage space furthest from your desk
Look at the storage space in your office. Assess what is in it. Any items that don't belong in your office should be removed and stored elsewhere. You may want to remove any items that you won't need to refer to again (like your tax records, for example), and put them somewhere that is part of your more 'inactive' living space, such as an attic or the garage. Allocate a time to clear one small section: a drawer or a shelf, for instance. Don't be too ambitious. It is important that you can finish what you start. You can always take on another shelf if you find you have the time. Throw away anything you don't need.

As usual, pick each thing up in sequence (to create a 'wake' of order) and make a decision as quickly as possible. Please do not let yourself start reading things any more than you need, to find out and categorise what they are. This is a particular temptation in an office, especially if you are of a social disposition and are clearing this area alone. A trick I sometimes use is to pretend that I'm going on holiday in half an hour and will miss the plane if I don't get through this pile of papers. Don't be tempted to defer decisions until later because you will end up with a mess that is neither sorted out, nor unsorted.

The questions to ask yourself as you clear out are:

- Do I still need this item and use it frequently? And when?
- Where do I tend to use it and how often? Replace it where you use it.
- Do I have to keep this? And if so, does it have to live with the 'active' items that are close to me in my office or could I put it somewhere else?

Only you know what is most relevant to you, which tasks you do most routinely, and which items you will need closest to you in order to do them. Use your own judgement here. You know what you are aiming to achieve. Sort anything you decide to put back in these storage spaces by category, and don't feel you have to fill all the space that has been created! Get rid of any stationery that you thought you would use but don't, or out-of-date flyers, posters, letterheads or information and old equipment manuals. Deal with the piles of paper on the floor next and don't forget to make a note of any tasks that you really have to do on your master list and to put anything

that needs dealing with in your in-tray. File and store what
you have to as far away from your working areas as is
practical (according to how often you will need to refer to
this material) and recycle or throw the rest out. Here are
some more ideas on how to deal with specific categories of
things as you encounter them.

■ Reading material
If you have stored lots of material for reading, which you
have never got round to, there are one or two things you
can do. Firstly, you could give yourself an amnesty and
discard or recycle it. You haven't suffered from not reading it so far and can probably survive without trawling
through it – I highly recommend this.

The other thing you can do is go through the material
(assuming this is trade journals, magazines or newspapers
we are dealing with) and tear out anything that is particularly relevant and put it in your in-tray to read later... If
you give yourself an amnesty but intend to stay on top of
your reading in the future, this is a good way to deal with
it as you go, so that you never acquire large unruly stacks
of things to read again. It's far more manageable than keeping whole magazines and having to search through them
again, having forgotten what it was you intended to look
at. What you can also do is to file all these cuttings in a
clear document folder in your pending tray, so that you can
grab them before a train journey or on the way to a meeting where you know you will be kept waiting. That way
you can catch up effortlessly. If your reading material

consists of books, then start a dedicated shelf so that you can reach for items here regularly.

■ Filing

Something that I resisted getting for a long time was a proper filing cabinet. I messed about, trying to make do with cardboard folders and concertina files for years. In the end, I found that I was resisting putting things away as much as I should have, either because I didn't really have enough room, or because it was a pain to go through all those folders in order to get the thing that I wanted out again when I needed it. Once I got a proper A4 filing cabinet with hanging files I never looked back. I think it is impossible to be properly organised without one. You will probably only need a two-drawer one to start with, and can put your printer on top of it so that it doesn't feel like wasted space. I also highly recommend this system because if you have concertina files instead, they multiply and you have to start remembering which one contains what... This defeats the purpose in the sense of reducing the amount of things that your poor brain has to remember. It is much better to have one roomy central system in which to file things.

How you label your files is up to you but it is often most useful to put the subject first and then any sub-headings afterwards. So if you are storing minutes from meetings with a specific client for instance, put 'X indus-tries/minutes'. If you started the file name with 'minutes...' but have lots of files devoted to minutes then you would have to trawl through all of them to find the minutes you want. Use a system that makes things easy to find. I have one drawer devoted to creative projects, one to domestic matters, one to business matters (such as correspondence, royalties and contracts, etc.) and one to personal growth and travel. This makes it easier for me to go to the right drawer first time, but in my case, no one else needs to access my files. Perhaps an alphabetical system might work better for you.

You may want to label computer or actual files with a date as part of the file name, but I think general subject, followed by a specific category, is easier to access. So 'company a/contracts' makes for less updating later when the time frame of some project or set of correspondence has shifted. It is also easier to read at a glance and to understand what the file contains. A final note of caution here is never to label a file 'Current'. It is just too big a subject and can become out of date too easily. Your in-trays (both real and virtual) will tell you what needs doing, as well as your master list.

Use your filing system to get things out of sight as much as possible. Now that you have your diary and to-do list to remind you to get your tasks done in a timely fashion, you don't need pieces of paper sitting on your desk and 'nagging' at you, in order to get things done. You can leave the papers you will need in the files until your diary or your master or project list triggers you to start working on them, and you can put them away at the end of the session, knowing that you will get them out again when you are next scheduled to work on that project. As I have stated earlier in the book, ironically being this tidy makes it more likely that you will feel like getting your project out again and finishing it, because going back to it only feels like going back to something partially complete, rather than something that looks like a mess... It will also force you to stop in a logical place before you put the project away if at all possible, and that can only make it easier to pick up the threads.

It is good standard practice to start a new folder for each project as you go, so that you have one central file into which you can toss all relevant information without thinking too hard about sub-categories. So, if you are writing several articles on different subjects, and having to interview experts piecemeal or research over a long period of time, then when you're ready to start on one, you only have to locate a single article file, because you sorted your material into project files as you went. This is still the same 'toothbrush principle' of storing everything needed for a particular task in a single 'workstation' location all together, only this time you aren't doing it with objects but with documents. Try to reduce the 'to file' pile to nothing now, and check that you really will need the items you decide to file, as you go. If not, throw them out!

■ Computer filing

You need to be just as tidy with the categorising of files within your computer if you want to make things easy for yourself. Always name new documents properly and clearly and put them in an appropriate file that will be a long-term home for them, creating these as you go. It only takes a second, and saves hours of trawling around opening file after file to see if it is the right one, later on, especially if there are several versions of the same document. This is especially important because the computer will try to save things with a title that suits its own logic but isn't necessarily that helpful to you.

You may need to spend a little time clearing up your filing within your computer and making sure that things are well and logically labelled. In addition, if you have two hard drives (and some models do divide their memory like this) then be sure that you are storing all the documents and files that you need to back up regularly, on the correct drive, and that your back-up system is set correctly.

■ Technology, passwords and 'spaghetti'
Do you have lots of cables and accessories for your computer, scanner, network, camera and mobile phone, etc.? Or your back-up hard drive, if you have one? Set aside a drawer for all these things. I find it useful to group them by the gadget they relate to, and put each of these groups of cables and plugs in its own resealable clear plastic bag, labelling it with an indelible marker. The sandwich bags that you can get from supermarkets and which people use on flights to carry their 100ml bottles of liquids are ideal for this. This way the leads don't get tangled or mixed up and you have an idea of what they are for and which set you can throw away if you upgrade a piece of

equipment. I also find it useful to keep a list of computer passwords (coded if necessary) with them. It is generally impossible to remember every single one. Alternatively, if you use Microsoft Word, you can create a Word document listing all these that you can lock by means of a password. When you save the document, click on 'tools' and then 'options'. Then click on the tab marked 'security' and fill in a password that you will be asked to confirm. Beware ... once you have done this you won't be able to access the document unless you know your password for it. It is easier to recall a single one, though, than the many you may use for every possible occasion.

■ Start creating 'zones'
When you have finished with all your sorting out (which may take you a good few clearing sessions) you can start moving the things you have left to the most convenient and efficient locations for them. You may have had a general area for storing all stationery but it is better to move each set of items now, to where they will be needed. So envelopes should be in your desk drawers if that's where you will use them, and plain and specialist papers by your printer. I suggest that you put pens, rulers, stapler in a top desk drawer (I am not a fan of leaving these items out on your desk) and blank CDs for burning in one lower down since you will need them less often. Notice that you don't have to store all the stationery together. That may look neat, but if it means that you have to walk across your office every time you want to print something, or you

need an envelope, it isn't efficient. Placing items like that will make everything seem laborious and make you feel less like starting tasks in the first place. Remember that image of you 'driving' your desk? Everything that you commonly need day to day should be at your fingertips. You shouldn't have to get up to get it. Remember to 'promote' and 'demote' things into their correct zones as you go.

■ Regular tasks
Do you need to do mail outs every so often (maybe once a month or less?) Create an area where everything you need to do that is in one place. Include the correct size of envelope, photos, printed information, brochures and stamps or whatever else you will need to accomplish the task. So if someone requests a pack, all you need do is go to that drawer, assemble it and address it. Think about your other regular tasks, particularly the ones on which you procrastinate. List them now, and use the same principle to arrange the materials you will need to do them, wherever you can.

■ Desk drawers
Start to clear out the desk drawers from the bottom up. This is so that as you get closer to that premium space in the upper drawers there is somewhere to demote the items you use less often. You now have such an easy-to-use filing system, and such clear storage spaces further away, that it will be easy to move items to where they are needed if they

don't belong here now. Is there anything that would be better stored near the printer? Or your mail-out drawer? Or which can be filed? Or put on a bookshelf? Or in your pending tray? Maybe this is a personal item and shouldn't really be there at all? Conversely, is there anything essential that you use every day, such as your calculator, which can be 'promoted' to your premium space?

■ Your desk

Finally, we get to the top of your desk! By now it should be easy to clear it of scraps of paper (or piles of it) that either belong in your in-tray or that, with a note on your master list, can be filed. All extraneous accessories can be removed and essential equipment put in desk drawers according to how often they are used. The only items that will remain on top of your desk are your desk trays, your computer, your desk lamp (well worth having so that you don't strain your eyes) and your phone. If there are lists or phone numbers that you constantly refer to, you may have a Rolodex or a notice board by your desk, on which these are pinned. This is also the place for any list of long-term goals that you have, so that you are reminded of what you are aiming for.

A special note here on 'inspiring things' such as ornaments, photos, etc. I do have these objects in my office, but I put them out of the way, on the walls or on top of bookshelves or cabinets. I don't put them where I need space to work. I recommend that you keep visual clutter to a minimum and that you do the same. The mind is too apt to be distracted and I think an office space is the one area where 'cosiness' and a 'busy' visual style doesn't really help.

It is tempting to think that you should site your computer right in the middle of your desk. This is where it always is in all those adverts, isn't it? (You know the ones paid for by computer manufacturers...) In fact you need space to make notes and to spread projects out that you aren't doing on the computer. So if you have the space to do it, put the computer to one side of the desk, where it is still easily accessible to work on, and leave some free space for old-fashioned thinking with pen and paper.

Take a minute to sit at your desk. It is clear and clean and you are in control. How do you feel? Remember this feeling and call it up whenever you have let things slide a little and need to rescue them.

■ Ongoing habits and commitments to yourself

Now you can start to have a clear desk all the time. You have arranged the space so that it is really easy to put things away, and also to know that they won't be forgotten. You have also got into the habit of dealing with no more than one matter at a time. So now you can make it a policy to clear as you go. Only get papers out which are relevant to the matter in hand. Deal with that task until you are finished (or finished with the stage of it that you are tackling for the moment) and put it away when you are done, and before you move on to the next thing. Make a note on your master or project list if you need to, to get it out again so that it doesn't get forgotten.

I find that it helps if I slow down, focus, enjoy feeling in control and to take deep breaths, on days where I am feeling tempted to flit from thought to thought or task to task. If you get into the habit of doing this when you sit at your desk, your mind will associate being at it with calm, concentrated, productive work, and will obligingly put you in this frame of mind every time you approach it. If you are aiming at reinforcing this effect, it is best only to work when you are feeling energised and to remember to take fresh-air breaks when you aren't.

If you put projects away as you go, you won't need to tidy your desk. It will be clear (with the exception of the thing you are currently working on) all day in any case. This is particularly useful if you are in a situation where you are constantly being interrupted or called away. If you do find yourself with a backlog, take five minutes to deal with it at the end of your work session. I like to take one last look at my desk as I put the lights out. It reminds me of how much I have accomplished that day and what a nice environment I have to come back to the next morning.

Try making a commitment to keeping things clear in this way for a month or so. You are going to do a daily check-in (if you committed to this in the previous chapter) and stick to your list. In addition to this, you are going to deal with one thing at a time and put things away as you go. How does it feel? Are you on top of everything? Does your system 'jam up' anywhere? Is there a surface that attracts junk? Or a category of things that tend to accumulate? As I have mentioned previously in the book, these are symptoms that point you towards minor problems in your system that need tweaking. Work out what is causing them and find solutions that you can establish easily, so that they don't occur again.

It should go without saying by now, that every new item or document that you bring into your office should be one about which you've made an initial decision. That is to say that you should know the correct place to put it immediately. Don't succumb to 'decision debt'.

■ Maintenance

Your office, just like every other system in your home, needs some basic maintenance. You will already have a routine to dust it regularly, but you will also need to have a routine for backing up your computer, debugging it of spyware (those tracking 'cookies' that many websites you visit try to plant in your computer in order to glean information about you), making sure that the anti-virus system is effective and up to date, and defragmenting the hard drive. You can get some programmes that will schedule in these tasks regularly and remind you or even run them without prompting in the background – set these systems up now.

Additionally, you will need to weed your paper files regularly, so that they don't get so full that you avoid doing the filing. Take it one drawer or even one file at a time, whatever works for you. Throw away as much as you can, archive as much as you can for storage in the attic or wherever, and create new files with subdivisions if one particular one is getting too fat with current material. Make a note in your diary to do this either every few months or once a year as is necessary.

If you are nervous about weeding files then the thing to bear in mind is that the areas near you in your office are premium space... You are the 'queen bee' (whatever your gender!) remember? If papers are going to sit in files near you, then they have to earn their keep by being things you are likely to want to refer to again. They may be maps or information on local or national travel (if this is something you have to do regularly). There may be a personal file that includes your passport, birth certificate and national insurance number. There may be a file with all your recent year-ending accounts summaries, or one which holds all your active bank accounts' terms and conditions and any passbooks. There may be current contracts, or working notes on long-term creative projects. Or there may be software discs and manuals for your electronic equipment. All the above are likely (allowing for updating of the information) to stay in your filing cabinet year after year. Correspondence may not be important and, if it's personal, for instance, and not that special, it can be thrown out once a year when you purge your files. Press cuttings or promotional material for your business may need to be kept but probably not near you (unless you want to show them to new clients), so if they are more than a year old, they can be moved to an archive folder wherever you keep these, possibly in your garage or attic. Catalogues for equipment, that was current when you filed them, but no longer is, can be thrown out.

Just remember to ask yourself:

- Will I need it again? Really? In which case do keep it ... and if it is legal or financial information and you are not sure, archive it just in case.
- When will I need it again? If this is less than a year from now, let it stay in the filing cabinet. If more than a year, banish it to the archive, labelling it clearly.

The big picture

The last thing we are going to do is look at the bigger picture. This is an optional exercise, but recommended. It will take about two hours of quiet uninterrupted time in total, and a pen and paper. If you have to break the exercise up, try to do parts 1 and 2 together. And try not to leave it too long before you get to part 3! You will need your enthusiasm to be fresh whilst you tackle it.

Part 1

Take a moment to close your eyes and think about what really inspires you. What makes you excited and energetic... Think about the things you would like to do, or to learn, or to experience. Think about the life you would love to have, and what you would need in order to get it. Let yourself dream. Remember all the things you loved to do at school or the hobbies you never made time to try, or the things you wanted to create, or the projects and dreamed-of experiences that friends or your parents told you were impractical.

Part 2

Write these down on a list. Then, narrow it down to the ones you are really excited about – the ones that you would be unhappy if you died without achieving. From these, pick two. If they are rather nebulous, decide how you will know when you have achieved them. If your goal is to be more assertive, work out how you will know when you have achieved this? If your goal is to be healthier, does that mean sleeping well or running a marathon? If it is to be rich, how much do you want to be earning a year? If it is to be glamorous, does that mean that you want to dress superbly, or that you want to get invited to all the best parties, travel extensively and socialise with lots of people in the arts? Make your two goals as measurable as you can and decide when, without putting too much pressure on yourself, you would like to have achieved them. In fact, it is useful to follow the SMART system below. Make your goals:

S pecific
M easurable
A chievable
R ealistic, and include a...
T imeline

Don't get too hung up about defining them perfectly. Start with a working definition that you can always refine as you go along, but try to incorporate all the SMART factors if you can.

Part 3

Write your two goals down neatly and pin them up near your desk. Whilst you are thinking about the time frame in which you would like to achieve them, start to break each of the two big goals down into sub goals, i.e. all the little steps it will take you to get there. For instance, if you want to work from home, to have and raise children, how long is it going to take you to achieve? Will you need to re-train? Or just get your current boss to allow you to do this? Will you need to research appropriate courses? Or maybe study and get qualified in another area? Or maybe build your own client base? Start a project file listing these steps and their time frames, and put the first ones on your master list. Prioritise these tasks. Try not to let weeks go by without you moving towards them. Set yourself a deadline, if necessary, and find yourself a buddy to help you stick to it.

If you find yourself procrastinating, ask yourself what scares you about achieving your dream and either modify your goal to take this into account or take steps to get past the emotional block, putting these on your project list. If you don't know how to get to your goal, make a list of people you can brainstorm with, or ask for advice. If one of your sub goals seems impossible, such as a residential course for your writing when you have children and can't leave them and can't afford it, break this down into further smaller steps and work towards them, dealing with one issue, such as childcare, at a time. Remember to track your progress on your project list or spread sheet, or regular check-ins with your 'buddy', and be honest with yourself about whether what you have achieved recently will help you reach that particular goal. You may have worked very hard, but if your work has no relevance to your goal, you will simply be doing what is required of you by others without ever getting closer to your cherished dream. Be honest with yourself about when you are letting other work get in the way of your making progress with what you truly want. How long are you going to wait to get it?

The important thing

You are important. Your dreams are important. They are what your life is really about, not your administration! The system you have set up should help you to stay on course with your larger aims and to delegate or jettison things, without neglecting the essential tasks that you have to do regularly. Don't let a lack of organisation, with either time or physical objects, stop you seeing and getting what you truly desire!

Chapter thirteen
Maintenance and troubleshooting

'I've tried clearing things out, but I still have to keep far more than I have space for in my 'heavy-traffic' areas. What can I do?'

If this is you, the crucial question to ask yourself when you are deciding if you really need to keep something in a high-traffic area is: 'When am I going to need it?' If you will need it in a few weeks or months and not every day and your space is very limited, then store it until you do. Vitamins and herbs are a good case in point. They are expensive but keep well and if you have a tendency to run low on a particular vitamin or mineral then you may realistically need it again. When you have some magnesium or Vitamin E or whatever, which you know is good for you occasionally but you're not taking at the moment, be ruthless and keep only what you need every day in the fridge or drawer in the kitchen. Put the rest in a box or crate and store it elsewhere until you decide to change your regime. You can create far more space around those 'premium' areas by doing this.

'I do a little bit of clearing at a time, but I
seem to end up creating new piles of stuff in
different places that I've cleared, and I'm
going round and round in a circle... I never
seem to get to a really tidy state even though
I'm putting in all this energy'

If you are seriously working to clear an area but seem to
be fighting a losing battle with the 'little and often'
approach, you can try several things. Firstly, do a very
specific visualisation with the space you are clearing.
Chances are that you haven't seen it 'complete' in your
mind's eye. I know you may have felt impatient with the
visualising chapter, but this is the reason you need it. If
you don't know what you are aiming for, your subconscious mind will resist change. It will feel, as you yourself
might, if I put you in my car and drove you somewhere at
70mph without explaining where we were going. Re-read
Chapter 3: Your Vision, and really see the space as you
wish it to look, either with eyes closed or open, whichever
works best for you. Make your picture very detailed, and
make sure it delights you. Then hold that image as you are
clearing out, as it will 'pull' you to completion. Without it
you are likely to get stuck.

If you are creating new piles in places you are still
clearing, remember that these are made up of new decision debts. You must cultivate the habit of making a
decision about where the object will be used, as you go,
because you will need this to maintain the space even
when you have finished clearing it. Re-read the points on

letting go of things, however 'useful' at some unspecified time (*perhaps in some alternative lifetime in a parallel universe, which you are not actually going to live right here? I can either be a concert pianist or a brilliant surgeon, not both... I may be equally suited to both, but if I'm going to be really good at either, I have to make a decision and plan accordingly. Yes, it's a waste, isn't it!*)

Lastly, it doesn't pay to stick to the easy corners to clear and to avoid the hard ones. You will simply be leaving problems for yourself to solve later. If you do, you will make it harder and harder to go back to clearing each time. In order to counteract this, your subconscious mind will get you to create little piles of stuff in areas you've already cleared, which are fairly easy to get rid of, so that you can clear the same area again and again. That way, you can avoid that corner you don't like the idea of clearing (with the really big and painful decisions that are waiting for you there) and avoid the knowledge that you're not getting anywhere because you're ducking the issue. So you can avoid the hard bits, feel virtuous and blame the system. Clever, eh! But is it getting you what you really want in the long term? If this is you, go back to clearing as you go along one wall, creating a 'wake' of order. Do not skip items! And do not reclutter areas you have cleared. Try to get to the point of having cleared the whole room so that you can establish new habits in there.

'I've read the book, but I really can't face getting started. I'm just not that methodical. But my chaos is driving me mad. There is too much stuff in my house and I can't move!'

Some people work better if they have an end goal and grand plan to get them there, or if they have a methodology worked out before they tackle a task. Others feel overwhelmed by that strategy because it seems to commit them to clearing the whole house in one go and that feels like too much. If you are a 'detail' rather than a 'whole picture' person, then the toothbrush principle will be difficult for you to implement. However, you can still make a start and an ongoing difference that builds up, by adopting this one set of four habits for a couple of weeks or a month, or whatever you can manage.

So every day:

1   Get rid of three things you no longer need (and I don't just mean your used milk cartons but something that has been hanging around getting in your way, even if it is out of a cupboard).

2   Relocate three things close to the exact spot where they will be used (taking care to see that they are easy to access).

3   When you use an item that *is* stored conveniently and correctly, take an extra few seconds to replace it there immediately when you've finished with it, every time.

4   Make a point of making decisions about anything new
    that gets brought into your home straightaway, and put
    it in the correct place for the task or bin it immediately.

Pay attention to how you feel as you see the space becoming clearer. Your initial inertia may be a symptom of a psychological issue that's holding you back, rather than that you are simply swamped or daunted. If it is, re-read the beginning of Chapter 3: Your vision, so that you can deal with it. If, on the other hand, you *are* simply swamped, but you can keep these new habits going for a while, then the chaos just has to melt away gradually. Even if your place doesn't look particularly tidy, you will still find that there is less to trip you up as you do your daily tasks.

'This system doesn't work! I organised things well initially, but small piles of stuff have started accumulating again...'

Have you noticed how sometimes a bend in a river (where the current slows down) will produce an accumulation of the detritus that has been floating in it? What you have been doing so far is carving out a new course for the river of energy in your home (by reorganising where things are stored) and speeding up the flow (by creating some good new habits so that things stay in their new places). It is, hopefully, far better than it was. But, although your house is no longer a stagnant pond, there will still be places where the flow slows down sometimes and things accumulate. We need to straighten out some of these tight bends, so that things keep flowing as they should.

What would you say the failures of the system in your house are, so far? Is there still a huge and growing pile of post on your kitchen counter? Do the children still leave all their toys around? Is the recycling spilling into everything else? Is your in-tray groaning? Make a list of all these small problems. Your job isn't quite over yet. These are the areas in which you didn't quite take all the factors into account the first time, or to which new factors have been added. The detritus is there to tell you exactly what needs tackling. The problem will be down to one of a few things. Either you haven't allowed enough storage for a function, such as the recycling, or what is more likely, you haven't noted one of your habits and accommodated it properly.

So if the post is building on the kitchen counter, it may be your habit to sort the post there over breakfast, or when you walk in after work. You can either change the habit or accommodate it. You can make a point of sorting the post in your office over your in-tray. Or you can provide yourself with a paper bin and an in-tray on the kitchen counter, which you take into your office when you see to all the household bills. If you do the latter you don't have to change your habit ... you will be able to sort the post out properly, put the paper in the recycling, and remind yourself of what needs tackling all in one go.

Do you need to reconcile yourself to the fact that you need more time for administration than you previously thought you did? Did you spend time throwing out the things you didn't need any more and reorganising the rest according to where they were needed, but not develop the habit of 'completion' (i.e. putting things away in the correct place immediately that you have finished the task)? Or did you let yourself bring new things into the house without making an initial decision about the task they were related to and where they should go? It is important to sort these tangles out now, one by one, rather than letting them build up and sabotage all your good work when you are so close. Remember clutter grows. A little begets a lot over time. Keep an eye on yourself because you are trying to make your instinct to put things away as you go automatic. You will need to do that religiously for at least a month before it is. Watch out for new habits and new functions that aren't quite working as you thought they would, as well. If you change the nature of your work and take on a whole new raft of projects, remember that your filing system will need to be updated. Hopefully, you will do that automatically, but if not and you find yourself avoiding the filing, stop to think about why. And then take action!

'Bundling'

A simple failure I noticed was that I kept buying hand cream and not using it, and my hands were getting rougher and rougher all the time. I tried putting it by the sofa thinking that I would use it when I was watching television. I tried putting it with my face cream to use before

I went to bed, but even though that was supremely logical I didn't find myself using it, and it was just becoming useless clutter. Finally, determined to make this new habit of moisturising my hands stick, I put it by the washbasin in the bathroom – for some reason that works for me. As soon as I dry my hands I find I apply the lotion, but it took a bit of working out.

The reason that it works is that I had found a good way of 'bundling' tasks together. In order to develop a new good habit, I tie it to a routine I already have, and which I have no trouble maintaining. Sometimes, it can take a bit of thought to work out the best thing to 'bundle' with, but it is worth the effort because the new habit is much more likely to become automatic quickly. You already bundle things such as going to the toilet (essential) and washing your hands (very much to be desired!), or feeding the cat in the morning and putting the kettle on for your first cup of tea. You also do it when you get into your car and check a whole list of things such as the handbrake, gear stick, mirror, seat position, etc., all at once. When you first started to drive, you had to remember to do these things singly, but now putting them all together is automatic.

Time

The other thing that you will notice is that over time, habits, interests and what is relevant to your everyday life changes. So your possessions need looking at every now and then and you need to do some 'weeding out' just to make sure that they are still relevant to the way you live and that they are stored in the most convenient places. This doesn't indicate failure any more than the need to empty your bins once a week does. It is just one of those things that has to be done occasionally and is far less traumatic if you do it in small bursts and regularly, before the need becomes truly pressing.

Tiredness

There are occasions when, although I have a system that works very well if I use it, I stubbornly *refuse* to, and things start to accumulate all over the place very quickly. For me, that is usually an indicator that I have allowed myself to become too tired, or that I am ill and need to cut myself some slack. If this is a chronic problem for you, consider whether you actually let yourself get far too exhausted every day to do things well and to maintain yourself (let alone a tidy house) properly. It is tempting to believe that we should be able to 'do it all' or even that some people do manage to 'do it all'. This is just not true. Sometimes you need to 'do nothing' or potter, without any pressure on yourself, so that you can recharge your batteries. Sometimes, you need to carve out rest time for yourself. You are no use to anyone else, no matter how much you love them, if you are tired and frazzled all the time. Assess what you are actually asking yourself to achieve and find a practical way of regularly offloading some of your tasks if you can. Most importantly, make creating time for yourself a priority.

Procrastination

Some people who understand this system and find that it works for them just cannot get it together to finish the initial organising, or to tackle the work that comes across their desk regularly enough ever to lose that 'hunted' feeling. They really want to but just can't seem to do it.

Procrastination can occur for many reasons and there are whole books written on the subject, but the likelihood, if the above description fits you, is that there is something about the process of clearing stuff away or being clear and organised that you don't like. Something that makes you feel uncomfortable. It may be that:

- You hate spending the time alone that it takes you to clear your clutter. Could you enlist a friend and schedule regular sessions with them until it is done?
- Or that when you are organised there are no excuses left and you're not allowing yourself to accept the fact that you're frightened, even by the prospect of a long-wished-for change... (I don't mind admitting that I feel frightened almost every day. I just won't let it stop me.)
- Or it may be that you've always had to be the 'sensible' or responsible one in your family and that actually

makes you very angry (in secret). Is the discomfort your rebellion causes you in your home worth it? And could you allow even one room to be an exception, just to see what that feels like?

- Or it may be that you actually hate having a tidy space. (Then don't have one!)
- Or that you fear that being tidy won't stimulate you enough and you won't be creative. Try grouping your visual stimuli into categories by project, and changing them regularly depending on what you are working on. You may find that being selective makes you *more* productive.
- Or it may be that you just have a bad case of FOMO (fear of missing out) and cannot bear to cut back on your social schedule, even temporarily, in order to get things cleared. Sometimes, you have to sacrifice a little to achieve a goal and miss out on some of the more immediate and fun stuff to do it. Is that something you constantly avoid doing? Only you can decide if being organised will save you enough time and effort in the long run to be worth it.

There are actually some very laudable reasons to procrastinate. If you have recently been bereaved, split with your partner, fallen in love or taken on more responsibility at work, your subconscious mind may have wisely decided that you actually need some proper 'down' time, where you do nothing, in order to cope with, or to fully enjoy/experience the special phase you are in. There are times when it's best to give yourself a break or deal with something that is more pressing.

What to do if you've never had a domestic routine

Some people have just never got around to establishing a domestic routine or hate the idea of one. If this is you, and you are ready to benefit from a bit more structure, then read on. Think of your time being divided much like your money. There is your savings or investment capital, which is meant to build up, and then there is your everyday spending money for rent or bills, which buys you heat, light, food and so forth for a short period, and which you will never see again.

Serious clearing time is designed to be like investment capital. But you will find that it doesn't build up as it should if you don't also have a chores routine every day to support it. What you will find instead is that the clearing you have done is steadily eaten away at, because you don't do your everyday tasks. That is much like not earning any everyday money and spending your savings instead. Not very wise! Set that to rights now.

Firstly, try to respect your own personal energy rhythms. We are not making this hard intentionally! So consider whether you have more energy at the beginning or the end of the day and work with this. If you like 'dream time' to read or think at the end of the day, why not do all the washing-up in one go after breakfast? That way you can leave the supper dishes in the sink without a conscience.

Tasks that may need to be done every day (depending on the size of your household) are:

- Washing-up/clearing kitchen.
- Laundry.
- Cooking dinner.
- Making packed lunches for yourself or your children.
- A small tidying session.

Try scheduling a 15- to 20-minute session for each of these tasks at a specific time of day. So after breakfast is a logical time to do the washing-up and laundry sessions. And when the dinner is cooking you have an obvious time slot that you can fill by making salads or sandwich fillings for the next day. If you put a single load of washing in the machine to do overnight, then you are set for the morning. You only need leave an extra half an hour in the morning and hardly any extra time in the evening if you would be hovering over the stove anyway. You only have to schedule a tidying session if you aren't completely religious about putting things away in their proper places as you go. Now is the time to make that habit concrete. If you don't you will be 'spending your savings' again.

Try giving yourself 15 minutes to do the washing-up and finish the task by wiping down whatever surfaces are clear in your kitchen with a cloth whilst you have your hands wet. Don't worry about surfaces that aren't, for the moment. As you clear more counter and table, they will become clear and get dealt with the next morning. Don't feel that you have to wash up or clean to the best possible standard. This isn't the time to get the steamer and the bleach out. The idea is to establish that you will do the routine *every day* and that it's quick and easy and no real hassle.

If you aren't used to a routine, after a day or so your subconscious mind will throw a tantrum. You *really* won't feel like doing it. Please don't give up at this point. Your subconscious mind is a toddler waiting to see if you will give way. If you don't, and you push through your resistance, it will give in and start helping you. You could try tying a set of tasks in with listening to your favourite radio show to keep you on track.

Once you have established the habit of putting things away as you go and doing your routine, you can start to schedule in an hour a day for serious clearing time. Try to make it the same time of day and every day so that your mind gets used to the idea. Remember, this is your investment and so the benefits (i.e. amount of clear space) should build up and build up. Beware doing too much at once and getting too tired, and stick to the golden rules. Clear logically, creating a 'wake' of order by dealing with the item in front of you whether 'easy' or 'hard'. Don't leave problems for later by letting yourself skip items. And each time you clear, come back to where you finished last time so that you build on what you did yesterday.

You can also have a weekly list of tasks such as:

- Clean the bathroom and change towels.
- Vacuum and dust.
- Change bed linen.
- Mow the lawn and tidy the garden.
- Do the grocery shopping.
- Do the ironing.
- Fill up the car with petrol (if relevant).

You can try assigning each of these to a specific day or doing them all on one day. Either way, knowing that you don't have to think about them because they are scheduled and you do them regularly, will keep you on top of things and feeling more peaceful and better able to relax.

If you're one of those people who work so hard that they hardly have enough time for sleep and a shower, let alone a domestic routine, then do some of the time-related exercises in the Chapter 11. You may find a way to permanently improve your time crunch by delegating, shedding tasks, or employing someone that can help on a regular basis.

Advanced projects

How is the system working for you? Have you been able to create some good new habits based on your natural 'completion' instincts? Now is the time to think about that

deep clean of your kitchen or bathroom or garage. It may
be the time to sort out the potting shed or greenhouse
before spring. The other thing to do now is look at your
scrap book again and think about redecorating or re-
accessorising, or buying some piece of furniture or gadget
that you now have space or time to use. When you do this,
remember to integrate it properly. Choose a good area in
which to locate it, and put everything else you will need
around it, at no more than arm's length away. Now that
your house is basically clear, you can also make it beautiful, comfortable and functional. The only limits are your
imagination and your budget.

Chapter fourteen
A final word

Have you managed to clear a room in your house and try out these new habits? Is that one area a reliable haven for you? Does it feel possible to have your home support you without too much effort? I do hope so, and that you are developing a quiet confidence about your ability to take control in your life and to create a peaceful sense of order wherever you go.

If you have learned more about your tastes and priorities from the first half of this book then I am happy for you. Congratulations if you have cleared a single room, or storage space. Even more well done, if you have been able to apply the 'function, zoning, and completion' principles effectively enough to that area, to ensure that it stays organised with very little effort. And if you have used the breathing space that being organised in there has given you, to look at what you would rather be doing, and created more of that in your life, then you are a master...

I leave you with a quote that sums up the way I think all of us instinctively feel about a well-ordered space.

'*Order functions to hold a space for us in which to do our life's work. Order creates a safe space in which the creative force within us can come forth. Order is a divine principle.*'

Taken from *Light Emerging* by Barbara Ann Brennan (Bantam New Age Books)

Appendix I
Five ways to build a new mindset

Forge your vision

Why do you want to clear your clutter? How will doing so enhance your life? What is your personal 'tidiness style'? 'Cosy' or 'minimalist'? Visualise the way your space will look when you have finished. How will you feel?

Deal with resistances

What are your personal 'downsides' to clearing your clutter? Is there anything that scares you about doing it? How can you take care of these concerns separately?

Debunk myths

What are your beliefs about living clutter-free and being well organised? Are they useful? Are they correct?

Cultivate good habits

Learn about the good instincts you already have. Discover how to harness them to develop habits that keep you well organised effortlessly.

The toothbrush principle

Understand the basic principles of 'zoning' and 'completion' that enable you to keep tabs on your toothbrush. Start to apply them more consciously and effectively to every item in your home.

Appendix II
The five principles to apply to clearing

Let go of 'things'

Questions to ask yourself:

- Do I need it? And when?
- Where do I tend to use it and how often?
- Does it enhance my life?
- Am I obliged to keep it for some reason?

Throw away, recycle or donate anything that doesn't fall into this category *as soon as possible*.

Repair any article that needs it and replace it in the correct zone *as soon as possible*.

Clear storage areas first, as a way of honing this skill, and to provide clear spaces for things that are not needed often. Store 'like with like' in true storage areas only, e.g. attics, not in cupboards that are part of your living spaces. Do a little often, rather than let yourself get tired.

Create zones

List all the functions of a room and all the tasks (whether for work or leisure) that you perform in it. List also where you do each of these tasks.

Start grouping all the things you need for each task in a 'zone' by order of frequency of use. Make additions or move furniture to help you do this if necessary, e.g. your reading light by your favourite armchair and bookshelf. Each function or task should have a zone where it is comfortable to perform that task and where everything is easily to hand and ready to go.

Create order as you go

Start by clearing the storage spaces in any room you're dealing with, first. Remember to let go of what you don't need, and place what you do in the zone where it will be used.

Pick up the first item and make a decision, then the next. Never skip an item. Do not defer decisions for later but work systematically, creating a 'wake' of order. Continue until the area concerned is clear. Put away relocated items in the correct zones.

Finish the session by taking items out to the bins or to be recycled or repaired. The session is not complete until you have done this.

Completion

When you do a task using any of the items in the zones you have created, take the extra three seconds it takes to put the item back in the correct place, ready to use again, *first time, and as you go*. Commit to this habit for two weeks. Make an instant decision when you bring any new item into the house, as to which 'zone' it should be located in and place it there.

Maintenance

Note down any areas where chaos reasserts itself and think about which functions and habits are not being allowed for. Correct these by setting the system up to allow for them.

New habits: 'bundle' these with established ones and organise items and spaces around them.

Request that others develop a new habit to make things easier where necessary. Make sure that the way you've arranged the items needed for the task makes this easy to do.

Acknowledgements

No one ever really gets anywhere on their own. When I look through the following list, I am still astonished at how freely and generously the people in it helped me as a new author.

In the first instance, it was Robert Best who, even in the face of my stubbornness, kept reminding me that I have talents other than singing and got me looking for them. I must thank Sue Roberts, who first asked me for help with her clutter and first suggested that I write a book. Shah Hussein provided essential inspiration and made me feel that I really could write one, even though I'd never written anything before, and in addition, the very good friends in my 'goals' group who egged me on, particularly Maya Preece, Lizzie Colman, Suzi Steer and Caroline Kenmore. So many friends, many of whom are also authors, have spent hours reading or brainstorming in order to give me much-needed feedback and support and advice, most notably, Lizzie Wingfield, Elinor Carter, Jo Waterworth, Nick Furze, Viv Andreae, Julie Picknell, Sanjida O'Connell and Joanna Crosse. Special mention must go to John Martineau of Wooden Books, who was ever ready to help with contacts, and to give encouragement and feedback, and some wisdom from the other side of the industry. In addition Alys Lewis and Caroline Turner at the literary department of Harbottle and Lewis were most patient and helpful.

I must also thank my agents, Jane Graham Maw and Jennifer Christie, from Graham Maw Christie, for their leap of faith in seeing potential in my book (and in me, when I had no track record as an author) and for finding a good home for it. Thanks to Chloe Darracot-Cankovic at the legal department of Random House, who was extremely gracious. Likewise to Miranda West at Vermilion Books for her enthusiasm for the project and for being that good home.

I am profoundly grateful to you.